COLLINS
DIY
GUIDE

PAINTING
& DECORATING

COLLINS

DIY

GUIDE

PAINTING
& DECORATING

JACKSON·DAY

HarperCollins*Publishers*

Published by
HarperCollins Publishers
London

**This book was created exclusively
for HarperCollins Publishers by
Jackson Day Jennings Ltd
trading as Inklink.**

Conceived, edited and designed
by Jackson Day Jennings Ltd
trading as Inklink.

Text
Albert Jackson
David Day

Editorial director
Albert Jackson

Text editors
Diana Volwes
Peter Leek

Executive art director
Simon Jennings

Design and art direction
Alan Marshall

Additional design
Amanda Allchin

Production assistant
Simon Pickford

Illustrations editor
David Day

Illustrators
Robin Harris
David Day

Additional illustrations
Brian Craker
Michael Parr
Brian Sayers

Photographers
Paul Chave
Michael Crockett
Michael Dunne
Clive Helm
Rodney Hyett
Albert Jackson
Simon Jennings
Ken Kirkwood
Neil Lorimer
Spike Powell
Tim Street-Porter
Jerry Tubby
Neil Waving
Peter Wolosynski

Picture researchers
David Day
Anne-Marie Ehrlich
Hugh Olliff

Proofreaders
Mary Morton
Alison Turnball

For HarperCollins
Robin Wood – Managing Director
Polly Powell – Editorial Director
Bridget Scanlon – Production Manager

First published in 1988
This edition published in 1995
Reprinted 1996

Most of the text and illustrations in
this book were previously published in
Collins Complete DIY Manual

ISBN 0 00 412768 4

Copyright © 1988, 1995
HarperCollins Publishers

**The CIP catalogue record for this
book is available from the British
Library**

**Text set in Univers Condensed
and Bodoni**
by Inklink, London

Imagesetting by
TD Studio, London

Colour origination by
Colourscan, Singapore

Printed and bound
in Hong Kong

Picture sources

Key to photographic credits
L = Left, R = Right, T = Top,
TL = Top left, TR = Top right,
C = Centre, UC = Upper centre,
LC = Lower centre, CL = Centre Left,
CR = Centre right, B = Bottom,
BL = Bottom left, BC = Bottom centre,
BR = Bottom right

almilmö Ltd: 16TR
Blue Circle Industries PLC: 49
Paul Chave:
8, IOT, 11T, 12, 42, 60L, 61
Michael Crockett/EWA: 9BL
Crown Berger Ltd: 14BL, 15TR, 33
Michael Dunne/EWA:
7BL, 9T, 13CL, 13CR
Faber Blinds (GB) Ltd: 7CR, 16BL
Gaskell Carpets Ltd: 60T
Clive Helm: 14TL, 16BR, 17TR
Rodney Hyett/EWA: 7TR, 14TR, 17BR
Albert Jackson: 7BR
Simon Jennings: 24, 26, 27, 28, 30
Ken Kirkwood: 7TL
Neil Lorimer: 10BR
Spike Powell/EWA: 17TL
Arthur Sanderson and Sons Ltd:
11BL, 14BR, 15BL, 15BR
Smallbone: 11BR, 15TL
Tim Street-Porter: 9BR
Jerry Tubby/EWA: 13T, 16TR
Neil Waving:
31, 36, 37, 44, 50, 51, 59, 60CR, 60BR, 61
Elizabeth Whiting Associates: 17TR
Peter Wolosynski/EWA: 13B, 17BL
Wrighton International Ltd: IOBL

CONTENTS

Cross-references
Since there are few DIY projects that do not require a combination of skills, you might have to refer to more than one section of this book. The list of cross-references in the margin will help you locate relevant sections or specific information related to the job in hand.

A BASIS FOR SELECTING COLOUR

Developing a sense of the 'right' colour is not the same as learning to paint a door or hang wallpaper. There are no 'rules' as such, but there are guidelines that will help. In magazine articles on interior design and colour selection you will find terms such as 'harmony' and 'contrast'; colours are described as tints or shades, and as cool or warm. These terms form a basis for developing a colour scheme. By considering colours as the spokes of a wheel, you will see how they relate to each other and how such relationships create a particular mood or effect.

Primary colours
All colours are derived from three basic 'pure' colours – red, blue and yellow. They are known as the primary colours.

Secondary colours
When you mix two primary colours in equal proportions, a secondary colour is produced. Red plus blue makes violet, blue with yellow makes green and red plus yellow makes orange. When a secondary colour is placed between its constituents on the wheel, it sits opposite its complementary colour – the one primary not used in its make-up. Complementary colours are the most contrasting colours in the spectrum and are used for dramatic effects.

Tertiary colours
When a primary is mixed equally with one of its neighbouring secondaries, it produces a tertiary colour. The complete wheel illustrates a simplified version of all colour groupings. Colours on opposite sides are used in combination in order to produce vibrant contrasting schemes, while those grouped on one side of the wheel form the basis of a harmonious scheme.

Warm and cool colours
The wheel also groups colours with similar characteristics. On one side are the warm red and yellow combinations, colours we associate with fire and sunlight. A room decorated with warm colours feels cosy or exciting depending on the intensity of the colours used. Cool colours are grouped on the opposite side of the wheel. Blues and greens suggest vegetation, water and sky, and create a relaxed airy feeling when used together.

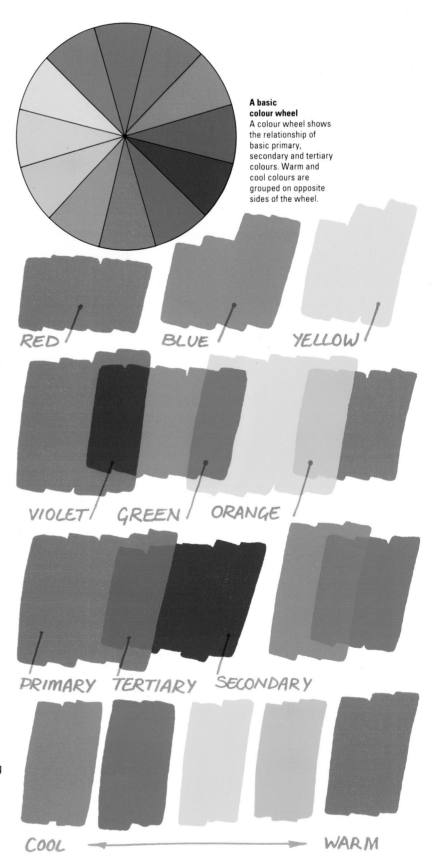

A basic colour wheel
A colour wheel shows the relationship of basic primary, secondary and tertiary colours. Warm and cool colours are grouped on opposite sides of the wheel.

RED

BLUE

YELLOW

VIOLET

GREEN

ORANGE

PRIMARY

TERTIARY

SECONDARY

COOL

WARM

A BASIS FOR SELECTING COLOUR

Bold treatment for a sitting room
(Top left)
A deep-red wall is made all the more striking by the use of a blue-painted ceiling and blue colouring in the curtains and upholstery.

A child's playroom
(Bottom left)
Primary and secondary colours, used in stylized and geometric forms, create a lively interior for a playroom.

Coloured equipment
(Top right)
Basic appliances such as sinks and radiators are now produced in a range of colours and play an important part in a colour scheme.

Adding colour with window blinds
(Centre right)
Coloured or patterned curtains are fairly commonplace, but fewer people choose from the available range of brightly coloured Venetian blinds. Strong sunlight contributes to the colourful effect.

Using colour outside
(Bottom right)
Most buildings do not lend themselves to being painted in bright colours. In areas of the country where colour is traditionally acceptable, a bold treatment can be very exciting.

USING TONE
FOR SUBTLETY

Pure colours can be used to great effect for both exterior and interior colour schemes, but a more subtle combination of colours is called for in most situations. Subtle colours are made by mixing different percentages of pure colour, or simply by changing the tone of a colour by adding a neutral.

Neutrals

The purest forms of neutral are black and white, from which colour is entirely absent. The range of neutrals can be extended by mixing the two together to produce varying tones of grey. Neutrals are used extensively by decorators because they do not clash with any other colour, but in their simplest forms they can be either stark or rather bland. Consequently, a touch of colour is normally added to a grey to give it a warm or cool bias so that it can pick up the character of another colour with which it harmonizes or provide an almost imperceptible contrast with a range of colours.

Tints

Changing the tone of pure colours by adding white creates pastel colours or tints. Used in combination, tints are safe colours; it is difficult to produce anything but a harmonious scheme whatever colours you use together. The effect can be very different, however, if a pale tint is contrasted with dark tones to produce a dramatic result.

Shades

The shades of a colour are produced by adding black to it. Shades are rich, dramatic colours which are used for bold yet sophisticated schemes. It is within this range of colours that browns appear – the interior designer's stock-in-trade. Brown blends so harmoniously into almost any colour scheme that it is tantamount to a neutral.

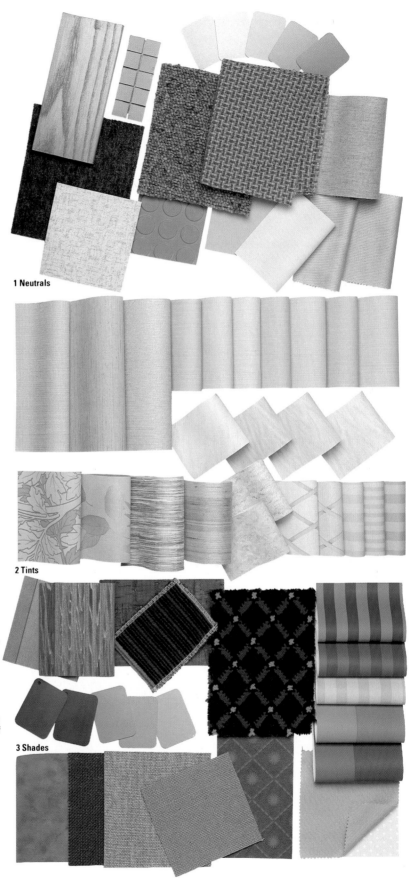

1 Neutrals

2 Tints

3 Shades

1 Neutrals
A range of neutral tones introduces all manner of subtle colours.

2 Tints
A composition of pale tints is always harmonious and attractive.

3 Shades
Use darker tones, or shades, for rich, dramatic effects.

USING TONE FOR SUBTLETY

White makes a spacious room
(Top)
Gloss white paint on the boarded ceiling and wall provides a light and refreshing dining room that is enhanced by the bright greens of the garden foliage beyond.

Using tints creatively
(Bottom left)
Pale colours are often used when a safe harmonious scheme is required, but you can offset them with the introduction of a strong neutral tone such as provided by the black cabinets on each side of this sofa.

Dark, dramatic tones
(Bottom right)
The very dark tone used for walls, ceiling and floors in this room is relieved by a painted frieze and white accessories. Gloss paint will reflect some light even when such a dark colour is used.

TAKING
TEXTURE
INTO ACCOUNT

Natural and man-made textures
(Right)
Many people are not conscious of the actual texture of materials. This selection ranges from the warmth of wood and coarsely woven materials to the smooth coolness of marble, ceramics, plastic and metal.

Textural variety
(Below)
It is relatively simple to achieve interesting textural variety with almost any group of objects. Here, a few stylish kitchen artefacts contrast beautifully with a patterned-tile splashback and warm oak cupboards.

Colour is an abstraction, being merely the way we perceive reflected wavelengths of light, yet we are far more aware of the colour of a surface than its more tangible texture, which we almost take for granted. Texture is a vital ingredient of any decorative scheme and merits careful thought.

The visual effect of texture is also created by light. A smooth surface reflects more light than one that is rough. Coarse textures absorb light, even creating shadows if the light falls at a shallow angle. Consequently, a colour will look different according to whether it is applied to a smooth surface or a textured one.

Even without applied colour, texture adds interest to a scheme. You can contrast bare brickwork with smooth paintwork, for instance, or use the reflective qualities of glass, metal or glazed ceramics to produce some stunning decorative effects.

Texture can be employed to make an impression, the source of which we may not even be consciously aware of. Cork, wood, coarsely woven fabrics and rugs add warmth, even a sense of luxury, to an interior, while smooth, hard materials such as polished stone, stainless steel, ceramic tiles, vinyl or even a black-lacquered surface give a clean, almost clinical feeling to a room.

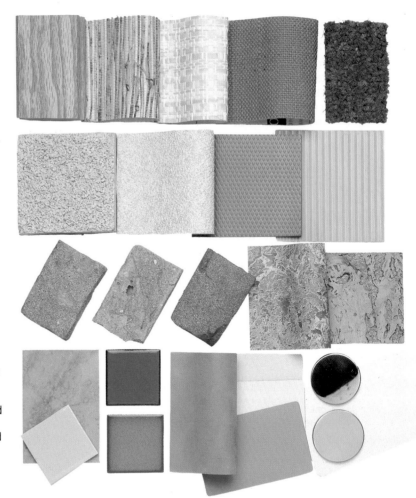

Carefully chosen textures *(Right)*
Soft and hard textures have been selected with care for this cool, sophisticated environment.

USING PATTERN FOR EFFECT

Recent purist approaches to design have made us afraid to use pattern boldly. Our less inhibited forefathers felt free to cover their homes with pattern and applied decoration with spectacular results, creating a sense of gaiety and excitement which is difficult to evoke in any other way.

A well-designed patterned wallpaper, fabric or rug can provide the basis for the entire colour scheme and a professional designer will have chosen the colours to form a pleasing combination. There is no reason why the same colours should not look equally attractive when applied to the other surfaces of a room, but perhaps the safest way to incorporate a pattern is to use it on one surface only to contrast with plain colours elsewhere.

Combining different patterns can be tricky, but a small, regular pattern normally works well with large, bold decoration. Also, different patterns with a similar dominating colour can coordinate well even if you experiment with contrasting tones. Another approach is to use the same pattern in different colourways. You should also select patterns according to the atmosphere you want to create. Simple geometric shapes are likely to be more restful than bold, swirling motifs.

Be bold with pattern
(Left)
There is no reason to be afraid of using pattern when you consider that manufacturers have done most of the thinking for you. Well-designed materials are available to clad just about any surface in your home.

Coordinated pattern
(Bottom left)
The colours used for the striped curtain and furniture fabrics are the basis of this coordinated colour scheme.

A profusion of pattern
(Bottom right)
This bedroom combines a wealth of pattern with the rich colour of natural-mahogany furniture. It shows what can be achieved if one has the courage to opt for the bold approach.

MANIPULATING
SPACE

There are nearly always areas of a house that feel uncomfortably small or, conversely, so spacious that one feels isolated, almost vulnerable. Perhaps the first reaction is to consider structural alterations like knocking down a wall or installing a false ceiling. In some cases such measures will prove to be the most effective solution, but there is no doubt that they will be more expensive and disruptive than the alternative ways of manipulating space by using colour, tone and pattern.

Our eyes perceive colours and tones in such a way that it is possible to create optical illusions that apparently change the dimensions of a room. Warm colours appear to advance, so that a room painted brown or red, for example, will give the impression of being smaller than the same room decorated in cool colours such as blue or green which have a tendency to recede.

Tone can be used to modify or reinforce the desired illusion. Dark tones, even when you are using cool colours, will advance, while pale tones will open up a space visually.

The same qualities of colour and tone will change the proportion of a space. Adjusting the height of a ceiling is an obvious example. If you paint a ceiling a darker tone than the walls it will appear lower. If you treat the floor in a similar way, you can almost make the room seem squeezed between the two. A long, narrow passageway will feel less claustrophobic if you push out the walls by decorating them with pale, cool colours which will, incidentally, reflect more light as well.

Using linear pattern is another way to alter our perception of space. Vertically striped wallpaper or woodstrip panelling on the walls will counteract the effect of a low ceiling. Venetian blinds make windows seem wider, and stripped wooden floors are stretched in the direction of the boards. Any large-scale pattern draws attention to itself and will advance like warm, dark colours, while from a distance small patterns appear as an overall texture so have less effect.

Practical experiments *(Right)*
A model will help to determine whether an optical illusion will have the desired effect.

Warm colours appear to advance

A cool colour or pale tone will recede

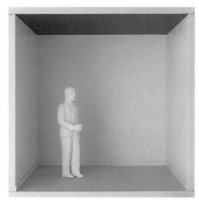
A dark ceiling will appear lower

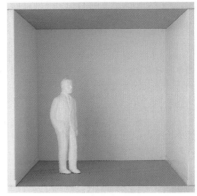
A dark floor and ceiling make a room smaller

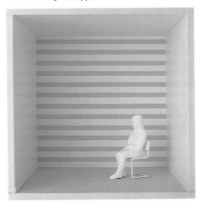
Horizontal stripes make a wall seem wider

Vertical stripes increase the height

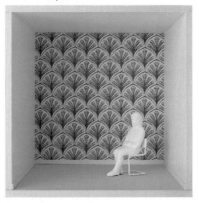
Large-scale patterns advance

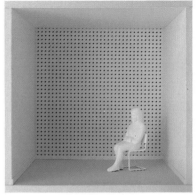
A small, regular pattern recedes

VERIFYING YOUR SCHEME

Before you spend money on paint, carpet or wallcoverings, collect samples of the materials you propose to use in order to gauge the effect of one colour or texture on another.

Collecting samples

Make your first selection from the more limited choice of furniture fabrics or carpets. Collect offcuts of the other materials you are considering, or borrow sample books or display samples from the suppliers to compare them at home. As paint charts are printed you can never be absolutely confident they will match the actual paint. Consequently, some manufacturers produce small sample pots of paint so you can make test patches on the wall or woodwork.

Making a sample board

Professional designers make sample boards to check the relative proportions of materials as they will appear in the room. Usually a patch of carpet or wallcovering will be the largest dominating area of colour, painted woodwork will be proportionally smaller and accessories might be represented by small spots of colour. Make your own board by gluing your assembly of materials to stiff card, butting one piece against another to avoid leaving a white border around each sample which would change the combined effect.

Incorporating existing features

Most schemes will have to incorporate existing features such as a bathroom suite or kitchen units. Use these items as starting points, building the colour scheme around them. Cut a hole in your sample board to use as a window for viewing existing materials or borrowed examples against those on the card.

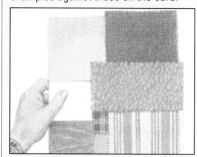

Checking your colour selection
View your completed sample board in natural and artificial light to check your colour selection.

SEE ALSO	
Details for:	
Colour theory	6-7
Tone	8-9
Texture	10
Pattern	11

Using mirrors
(Top)
Mirrored wardrobe doors fitted from floor to ceiling provide the illusion of a larger space.

Lowering a ceiling
(Centre left)
A dark-tone ceiling reduces the apparent height of the room and also helps disguise supporting beams.

Creating space in a hallway
(Centre right)
A trompe l'oeil glazed door with a garden vista beyond creates an illusion of space in a confined area.

Creating space with pattern
(Bottom)
The linear effects of patterned carpet and pictures ranged across the wall help to make this room seem larger.

13

SCHEMES FOR LIVING ROOMS

In most homes the living room is the largest area in the house. It is where you spend most of your leisure time and entertain your friends, and the room upon which most money is spent in terms of furnishings, curtains and carpets, not to mention expensive hi-fi units, the television set and so on. For all these reasons, you will want to make sure that the living-room decor has lasting appeal. After all, you are unlikely to replace costly furniture and materials frequently.

Unless you are lucky enough to have more than one reception or living room, it is an area that must feel comfortable during the day, relaxing in the evening and lively enough for the occasional party. If the room receives very little sunlight, a warm colour scheme is often the best in order to create a cosy atmosphere. Dark, cool tones will produce a similarly snug result under artificial light, but very deep tones can have the opposite effect by creating dark, shadowy areas. Neutral colour schemes or a range of browns and beiges will be easy to change in the future by simply swapping the accessories without having to spend money on replacing essentials. Natural textures are equally versatile.

Patterned carpets or rugs are less likely to be ruined by the inevitable spillages than plain colours, but very dark tones are almost as difficult to keep clean as pale colours.

Curtains and blinds provide the perfect solution to a change of mood. During the day they are pulled aside or rolled up and therefore contribute very little to the general appearance of the room, but in the evening they can become a wall of colour or pattern which can transform the scheme.

Sheer curtains or blinds can also be used to screen the view through the window while allowing daylight to fill the room with a soft light that will not damage upholstery fabrics.

Sympathetic style
(Top left)
A surviving period living room deserves appropriate styling.

Simple styling suits a modern house
(Top right)
A modern home can be treated successfully with restrained colours and natural textures.

An adaptable scheme
(Bottom left)
A safe yet comfortable scheme lends itself to change by swapping the accessories.

Typically traditional
(Bottom right)
Pink-washed walls and floral patterns suit a typical country cottage.

SCHEMES FOR
BEDROOMS

A bedroom is first and foremost a personal room. Its decor should reflect the character of its occupant and the functions to which the room is put. At night, a bedroom should be relaxing, even romantic. Much depends on the lighting, but pattern and colour can in themselves create a luxurious and seductive mood.

Few people ever use pattern on a ceiling yet a bedroom provides the ideal opportunity, especially as you are unlikely to spend much of your waking life there and can consequently afford to be adventurous with the decor. Bedroom carpet is invariably of inferior quality because it need not be hardwearing, but you could give the colour scheme a real lift by investing in an expensive rug or deep-pile carpet knowing that it will come to no harm. If a bedroom faces south early sunlight will provide the necessary stimulus to wake you up, but a north-facing room will benefit from bright, invigorating colours.

Some bedrooms may have to serve a dual function. A teenager's bedroom, for example, may have to double as a study or a private sitting room so needs to be stimulating rather than restful. A child's bedroom will almost certainly function as a playroom as well. The obvious choice would be for strong, even primary colours, but as most children accumulate large numbers of brightly coloured toys, books and pictures you might select a neutral background to the colourful accessories. The smallest bedrooms are usually reserved for guests, but they can be made to appear larger and more inviting by the judicious manipulation of the proportions with colour or tone.

An elegant master bedroom
(Top left)
This elegant bedroom has a peaceful character, created from a basically neutral scheme warmed very slightly by a hint of cream and pale yellow.

Bright and refreshing
(Top right)
The combination of bright yellow and white makes for a cheerful and lively start to the day.

Dual-purpose room
(Bottom left)
When a bedroom doubles as a sitting room it needs to be stimulating during the day and cosy at night.

A guest room
(Bottom right)
A guest room should make a visitor feel at home immediately. The warmth of stripped pine makes this room very inviting.

15

DECOR FOR COOKING AND EATING

Kitchens need to be functional areas capable of taking a great deal of wear and tear, so the materials you choose will be dictated largely by practicalities. However, that does not mean you have to restrict your use of colour in any way. Kitchen sinks and appliances are made in bright colours as well as the standard stainless steel and white enamel, while tiled worktops and splashbacks, vinyl floor coverings and melamine surfaces offer further opportunity to introduce a range of colours.

Textures are an important consideration with a range of possibilities. Natural timber remains a popular material for kitchen cupboards and will provide a warm element which you can either echo in your choice of paint, paper or floorcovering or contrast with cool colours and textures. Some people prefer to rely entirely on plastic, ceramic and metallic surfaces which give a clean and purposeful character.

If the kitchen incorporates a dining area you may decide to decorate the latter in a fashion more conducive to relaxation and conversation. Softer textures such as carpet tiles, cork flooring and fabric upholstery absorb some of the clatter that is generated by kitchen utensils. You could also decorate the walls in a different way to change the mood, perhaps using darker tones or a patterned wallcovering to define the dining area.

A functional kitchen
(Top left)
This simple kitchen, laid out to form a perfect work triangle, looks extremely functional without feeling clinical.

A family kitchen
(Top right)
Some people like the kitchen to be part of an informal sitting and dining area where the family can relax.

A breakfast room
(Bottom left)
A sunny alcove linked to the kitchen makes an ideal area for a breakfast room.

A kitchen extension
(Bottom right)
Colourful fabric blinds shade this kitchen extension from direct sunlight.

BATHROOMS

Bathrooms, like kitchens, must fulfil quite definite functions, but they should never look clinical. Even when a bathroom is centrally heated a cold, uninviting colour scheme would not be a wise choice as enamelled and tiled surfaces are inevitable. Coloured bathroom appliances are commonplace, but choose carefully as they are likely to remain the dominating influence on any future colour schemes.

Like the bedroom, the bathroom is an area where you can afford to be inventive with your use of colour or pattern. A bold treatment which might become tiresome with overexposure can be highly successful in a room used only for brief periods. Try to introduce some sound-absorbing materials such as ceiling tiles, carpet or cork flooring to avoid the hollow acoustics associated with old-fashioned tiled bathrooms. If you want to use delicate materials that might be affected by steam, make sure that the bathroom is

properly ventilated. Bathrooms are usually small rooms with relatively high ceilings, but painting a ceiling a dark tone that might improve the proportion of a larger room can make a bathroom feel somewhat like a box. A more successful way to counter the effect of a high ceiling is to divide the walls with a dado rail, using a different colour or material above and below the line.

If your home is in a hard-water area, avoid dark-coloured bathroom suites which will inevitably emphasize ugly lime-scale deposits.

Changing the proportion
(Top left)
The use of a wood-panelled dado reduces the apparent height of this bathroom and introduces a warm, attractive texture to the interior.

Pure white
(Top right)
A woven-cane chair and delicate potted plants relieve the stark qualities of this all-white bathroom.

Warm and luxurious
(Bottom left)
There is no reason why your bathroom should not be designed and furnished in the style of an elegant sitting room.

Fashionable styling
(Bottom right)
The blue stained glass of the original window has been used as the basis for the colour scheme of this period-style bathroom.

17

MEANS
OF ACCESS

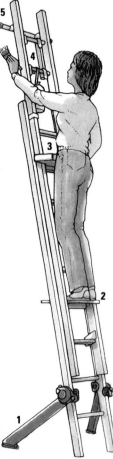

Ladder accessories
Kit out your ladder with a range of helpful devices to make working easier and safer. This ladder features stabilizers (1) for uneven ground, a foot rest for comfort (2), a tool tray (3), a paint-can hook (4) and a stay (5) to hold the top away from eaves or gutters.

BEFORE YOU BEGIN

Timing, weather and the condition of the site are important factors to consider before you decorate outside. Indoors, you have the problem of what to do with a room full of furniture and furnishings while you work.

Outside the house

Plan your work so that you can begin the decoration of the house exterior in late summer and autumn when the previous warm weather will have dried out the fabric of the building sufficiently.

The best weather for decorating is a warm but overcast day. Avoid painting on rainy days or in direct sunlight, as both rain and sun can ruin new paintwork. On a sunny day, follow the sun around the house so that its warmth will have dried out the night's dew on the woodwork before you apply paint.

Do not work on windy days or dust will be blown on to the paint. Sprinkle water or spray it with a houseplant spray around doors and windows before you paint to settle dust which would otherwise be churned up by your feet.

Clear away any rubbish around the house, as it will slow your progress and may even cause accidents. Cut back overhanging foliage from trees and shrubs. Protect plants and paving with dustsheets in the work area.

Inside the house

Before you decorate a room inside, carry out all repairs necessary and have the chimney swept if you use an open fire: a soot fall would ruin your decorations. Clear as much furniture from the room as possible, and group what is left under dustsheets. Lift rugs or carpets, then spray water on the floor and sweep it to collect dust before you begin to paint. Protect finished wood or tiled floors with dustsheets.

Remove all furnishings such as pictures and lampshades, and unscrew fingerplates and door handles. Keep the access door handle in the room with you in case you accidentally get shut in.

What to wear

Do not wear woollen garments when decorating as they tend to leave hairs sticking to paintwork. Overalls with loops and large pockets for tools are ideal for decorating and other work.

Whether you are decorating inside or out, you must provide adequate means of reaching the area on which you are working. Using inefficient equipment and makeshift structures is dangerous; even if you do not want to buy suitable ladders, you can hire them quite cheaply. Safety and comfort while working are important considerations, and there is a range of devices and accessories to make the job that much easier.

Types of ladders and access equipment

Stepladders are essential for interior decoration. Traditional wooden stepladders are still available, but they have been largely superseded by lightweight aluminium-alloy types. You should have at least one that stands about 2m (6ft 6in) high so that you can reach a ceiling without having to stand on the top step. A second shorter ladder might be more convenient for other jobs and you can use both, with scaffold boards, to build a platform.

Outdoors you will need ladders to reach up to the eaves. Double and triple wooden extension ladders are very heavy, so consider a metal one.

Some doubles and most triples are operated by a rope and pulley so that they can be extended single-handed.

To estimate the length of ladder you need, add together the ceiling heights of your house. Add at least 1m (3ft 3in) to the length to allow for the angle and access to a platform.

There are many versions of dual-purpose or even multi-purpose ladders which convert from stepladder to straight ladder. A well-designed, versatile ladder is a good compromise.

Sectional scaffold frames can be built up to form towers at any convenient height for decorating inside and outside. Wide feet prevent the tower sinking into the ground, and adjustable versions allow you to level it. Some models have locking castors, which enable you to move the tower.

Towers are ideal for painting a large expanse of wall outdoors. Indoors, smaller platforms made from the same scaffold components bring high ceilings within easy reach.

Accessories for ladders

● **Ladder stay** A stay holds the ladder away from the wall. It is an essential piece of equipment when painting overhanging eaves and gutters: you would otherwise be forced to lean back, risking overbalancing.
● **Tool tray and paint-can hook** You should always support yourself with one hand on a ladder, so use a wire or bent-metal hook to hang a paint can or bucket from a rung. A clip-on tray is ideal for holding a small selection of tools.

● **Clip-on platform** A wide flat board, which clamps to the rungs, provides a comfortable platform to stand on while working for long periods.
● **Stabilizers** Bolt-on accessories that prevent the ladder from slipping and compensate for uneven ground.

Alloy stepladder   **Dual-purpose ladder**   **Scaffold tower**   **Extending ladder**

When you buy or hire a ladder, either wooden or metal, bear in mind that:
● Wooden ladders should be made from straight-grained, knot-free timber.
● Good-quality wooden ladders have hardwood rungs tenoned through the upright stiles and secured with wedges.
● Wooden rungs with reinforcing metal rods stretched under them are safer than ones without.
● End caps or foot pads are an advantage to prevent the ladder from slipping on hard ground.
● Adjustability is a prime consideration. Choose a ladder that will enable you to gain access to various parts of the building and will convert to a compact unit for storage.
● The rungs of overlapping sections of an extension ladder should align or the gap between the rungs might be too small to secure a good foothold.
● Choose an extension ladder with a rope and pulley, plus an automatic latch that locks the extension to its rung.
● Check that you can buy or hire a range of accessories (see opposite) to fit your make of ladder.
● Choose a stepladder with a platform at the top to take cans and trays.
● Treads should be comfortable to stand on. Stepladders with wide, flat treads are the best choice.
● Stepladders with extended stiles give you a handhold at the top of the steps.
● Wooden stepladders often have a rope to stop the two halves sliding apart. A better solution used on most metal stepladders is a folding stay, which locks in the open position.

Is the ladder safe to use?

Check ladders regularly and before you use them after a winter's break. Inspect a hired ladder before use.

Look for splits along the stiles and check that there are no missing or broken rungs and that the joints are tight. Sight along the stiles to make sure they are aligned, or the ladder could rock when leant against a wall.

Inspect wooden ladders for rot or woodworm. Even a small amount of sponginess or a few holes could signify serious damage below the surface. Test that the wood is sound before using the ladder and treat it with a preserver or woodworm fluid. If in doubt, scrap the ladder for safety's sake.

Check that fixings for hinges and pulleys are secure and lubricate them. Inspect the pulley rope for fraying and renew if necessary.

Oil or varnish wooden ladders regularly to stop them drying out. Apply extra coats to the rungs, which take most wear. Do not paint a ladder as this may hide serious defects.

How to handle a ladder

Ladders are heavy and unwieldy; handle them properly so that you do not damage property or injure yourself.

Carry a ladder upright, not slung across your shoulder. Hold the ladder vertically, bend your knees slightly, then rock the ladder back against your shoulder. Grip one rung lower down while you support the ladder at head height with your other hand, then straighten your knees.

To erect a ladder, lay it on the ground with its feet against the wall. Gradually raise it to vertical as you walk towards the wall. Pull the feet out from the wall so that the ladder is resting at an angle of about 70 degrees – if the ladder extends to 8m (26ft) for example, its feet should be 2m (6ft 6in), or one-quarter of its height, from the wall.

Raise an extending ladder to the required height while holding it upright. If it is a heavy ladder, get someone to hold it while you operate the pulley.

Handling a ladder
Carry the ladder upright, leaning back against your shoulder; grip one rung low down, another at head height. When erected, the base of the ladder should be one-quarter of its height away from the wall so that it is correctly balanced.

WORKING
WITH LADDERS

HOW TO USE
A LADDER SAFELY

More accidents are caused by the unwise use of ladders than by faulty equipment. Erect the ladder safely before you ascend it and move it when the work is out of reach – never lean to the side or you will overbalance. Follow these simple, commonsense rules:

Securing the ladder
If the ground is soft, spread the load of the ladder by placing a wide board under the feet; screw a batten across the board to wedge the ladder in place. On hard ground, make sure the ladder has anti-slip end caps and lay a sandbag (or a tough polyethylene bag filled with earth) at the base.

Secure the stiles near the base with rope tied to timber stakes driven into the ground at each side and just behind the ladder (**1**). When you extend a ladder the sections should overlap by at least one-quarter of their length. Do not lean the top against gutters, soil pipes, drainpipes and, especially, glass as they may give way.

Anchor the ladder near the top by tying it to a stout timber rail, held across the inside of the window frame. Make sure that the rail extends about 300mm (1ft) on each side of the window and pad the ends with old cloth to protect the wall from any damage (**2**).

It is a good idea to fix ring bolts at regular intervals into the masonry just below the fascia board: this is an excellent way to secure the top of a ladder as you will have equally good anchor points wherever you choose to position it. Alternatively, fix large screw eyes to the masonry or a sound fascia board and attach the ladder to them.

Safety aloft
Never climb higher than four rungs from the top of the ladder or you will not be able to balance properly and there will be no handholds within reach. Keep both your feet on a rung and your hips centred between the stiles. Avoid a slippery foothold by placing a sack or doormat at the foot of the ladder to dry your boots before you ascend.

Unless the manufacturer states otherwise, do not use a ladder to form a horizontal walkway, even with a scaffold board lying on it.

Stepladders are prone to topple sideways. Clamp a strut to the stile on uneven floors (**3**).

1 Staking a ladder
Secure the base of the ladder by lashing it to stakes in the ground.

2 Securing the top
Anchor the ladder to a batten held inside the window frame.

3 Supporting a stepladder
Clamp a strut to the stile to prop up a pair of stepladders.

19

ERECTING
WORK
PLATFORMS

A lot of work can be carried out by moving a ladder little by little as the work progresses. However, this can become tedious and may lead to an accident as you try to reach just a bit further before having to move along; you will find it more convenient to build a work platform that allows you to tackle a large area without moving the structure. You can hire decorators' trestles and bridge a pair with a scaffold board, or make a similar structure with two pairs of stepladders (1).

Clamp or tie the board to the rungs and use two boards, one on top of the other, if two people need to use the platform at once.

An even better arrangement is to use scaffold-tower components to make a mobile platform (2). One with locking castors is the ideal solution for painting or papering ceilings.

2 Mobile platform
An efficient structure made from scaffold-tower frames.

1 Improvised platform
A simple yet safe platform made from stepladders and a scaffold board.

Gaining access to a stairwell

Stairwells present particular problems when you are building work platforms. The simplest method is to use a dual-purpose staircase ladder, which can be adjusted to stand evenly on a flight (3). Anchor the steps with rope through a couple of large screw eyes fixed to the stair risers; the holes will be concealed by carpet later. Rest a scaffold board between the ladder and the landing to form a bridge. Screw the board to the landing and tie the other end.

Alternatively, construct a tailor-made platform from ladders and boards to suit your staircase (4). Make sure the boards and ladders are clamped or lashed together, and that the ladders cannot slip on the treads. If necessary, screw wooden battens to the stairs to prevent the foot of the ladder moving.

Stair scaffold
Erect a platform with scaffold frames to compensate for the slope of a staircase .

3 Dual-purpose ladder
Use a stair ladder to straddle the flight with a scaffold board to give a level work platform.

Cloths protect wall

Boards lashed together

Screwed to box

Battens screwed to landing

4 Tailor-made platform
Build a network of scaffold boards, stepladders, ladders and boxes to suit your stairwell layout.

ERECTING
PLATFORMS OUTSIDE

Scaffolding is by far the best method of building a work platform to decorate the outside of a house. Towers made from slot-together frames are available for hire. Heights up to about 9m (30ft) are possible; the tallest ones require supporting 'outriggers'.

Build the lower section of the frame first and level it with adjustable feet before erecting a tower on top. As you build, climb up and stand on the inside of the tower.

Erect a proper platform at the top with toe boards all round to prevent tools and materials being knocked off and extend the framework to provide hand rails all round. Secure the tower to the house by tying it to ring bolts fixed into the masonry, as with ladders.

Some towers incorporate a staircase inside the scaffold frame; floors with trapdoors enable you to ascend to the top of the tower. If you cannot find such a tower, the safest access is via a ladder. Make sure it extends at least 1m (3ft 3 in) above the staging so that you can step on and off safely.

It is difficult to reach windows and walls above an extension with just a ladder. With a scaffold tower, however, you can construct a cantilevered section fixed to the main tower which rests on the roof of the extension.

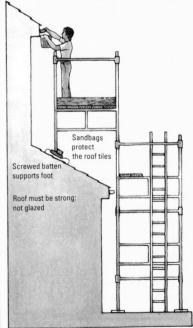

Sandbags protect the roof tiles

Screwed batten supports foot

Roof must be strong: not glazed

Erecting a cantilevered platform
Rest cantilever section on a board to spread the load.

PREPARATION AND PRIMING

Thorough preparation of all surfaces is the vital first step in redecorating. If you neglect this stage, subsequent finishes will be rejected. Preparation means removing dirt, grease and loose or flaking finishes, as well as repairing serious deterioration such as cracks, holes, corrosion and decay. It is not just old surfaces that need attention: new timber and metalwork must be sealed for protection, and priming is necessary to ensure a surface is in a suitable condition to accept its finish. Consult the charts on this page for details of primers and sealers for all the materials you are likely to encounter in and around the home, then read the following sections, which examine each material in detail.

TYPES OF PRIMERS AND SEALERS

There are numerous primers and sealers to suit a variety of materials.

Stabilizing primer
Used to bind powdery or flaky materials. A clear or white liquid.

Wood primer
Standard solvent-based pink or white primer prevents other coats of paint soaking in.

Acrylic wood primer
Fast-drying water-based primer. Some types can be used for undercoating.

Aluminium wood primer
Used to seal oily hardwoods, it will also cover creosote.

General-purpose primer
Seals porous building materials and covers patchy walls and ceilings.

Metal primers
Essential to prevent corrosion in metals and to provide a key for paint. Special rust-inhibitive primers both treat rust and prevent its recurrence.

PVA bonding agent
A general-purpose liquid adhesive for many building materials. An excellent primer and sealer when diluted, even for bituminous paints.

Water repellent
A liquid which dries colourless and is used to seal masonry against water penetration.

Alkali-resistant primer
Used to prevent the alkali contents of some materials attacking oil paints.

Aluminium spirit-based sealer
Formulated to obliterate materials likely to 'bleed' through subsequent coatings. Effective over bituminous paints, metallic paints, creosote and nicotine.

SEE ALSO
Details for:
Priming plaster — 22
Priming wood — 27
Priming metal — 30

● Black dot denotes that primer and surface are compatible.

● Red dot denotes metal primers

● **Lead content in paint**
Lead, which is a poison, was widely used in the past as a dryer in solvent-based paints, including primers. (Emulsions, which are water-based, have never contained lead). Most solvent-based paints are now made without lead. If possible, choose one labelled 'no lead added' or similar. Do not let children chew old painted surfaces, which may have a high lead content.

PRIMERS AND SEALERS: SUITABILITY, DRYING TIME AND COVERAGE

SUITABLE FOR	Stabilizing primer	Wood primer	Acrylic wood primer	Aluminium wood primer	General-purpose primer	Zinc-phosphate primer	Fast-drying metal primer	Rust-inhibitive primer	PVA bonding agent	Water repellent	Alkali-resistant primer	Aluminium spirit-based sealer
Brick	●				●				●	●	●	
Stone	●				●				●	●	●	
Cement rendering	●				●				●	●	●	
Concrete	●				●				●	●	●	
Plaster	●				●				●		●	
Plasterboard	●				●						●	
Distemper	●											
Limewash	●											
Cement paint	●											
Bitumen-based paints									●			●
Asbestos cement	●				●						●	
Softwoods/hardwoods		●	●	●	●							
Oily hardwoods				●								
Chipboard		●	●	●	●							
Hardboard		●	●	●	●							
Plywood		●	●	●	●							
Creosoted timber				●								●
Absorbent fibre boards	●										●	
Ferrous metals (inside)						●	●	●				
Ferrous metals (outside)						●	●	●				
Galvanized metal						●						
Aluminium						●						
DRYING TIME: HOURS												
Touch dry	3	4-6	0.5	4-6	4-6	4	2	2	3	1	4	0.25
Recoatable	16	16	2	16	16	16	5-6	6	16	16	16	1
COVERAGE (Sq m per litre)												
Smooth surface	6	12	12	13	12	13	8	8	9	3-6	10	4
Rough/absorbent surface	7	10	10	11	9	10	6	6	7	2-3	7	3

PLASTERWORK: MAKING GOOD

Plaster is used to finish the inner surfaces of the walls and ceilings in most houses. Ceilings are traditionally clad with slim wood laths which are then plastered over: the plaster grips between the laths. Walls are usually covered directly with a backing (floating) coat of plaster and a smooth finish coat, various grades of plaster being used to suit the condition and quality of the masonry. An old house might have lath-and-plaster walls and ceilings; in modern houses, plasterboard is used instead. A plastered or boarded surface can be decorated with paint, paper or cladding such as tiles, the preparation being similar for each. Whatever you intend to use as a decorative finish, the plastered wall or ceiling must be made good by filling cracks and holes.

Smooth finish
Smooth the surface of small repairs with a wet brush or knife in order to reduce the amount of sanding required later.

PREPARING TO DECORATE

New plaster

Before you decorate new plaster, allow efflorescence to form on the surface, then wipe it off with sacking; repeat periodically until it ceases to appear.

For brand-new interior surfaces use new-plaster emulsion only; standard vinyl emulsions are not sufficiently moisture-vapour permeable. Always leave fresh plaster to dry out thoroughly before decorating with wallpaper or any paint other than new-plaster emulsion. Use an alkali-resistant primer first if you are applying solvent-based paints. Size new, absorbent plaster before hanging wallpaper or the water will be sucked too quickly from the paste, which will result in poor adhesion. Use either a proprietary size or a heavy-duty wallpaper paste. If you are hanging vinyl wallcovering, make sure that the size contains fungicide as vinyl cannot breathe like a plain paper can.

For tiling, no further preparation is needed once the plaster is dry.

Old plaster

Apart from filling minor defects and dusting down, old, dry plaster needs no further preparation. If the wall is patchy, apply a general-purpose primer.

If the surface is friable apply a stabilizing solution before you decorate.

Do not decorate damp plaster; cure the fault, then let the plaster dry out.

Plasterboard

Fill all joints between newly fixed plasterboard, then, whether you are painting or papering the board, daub all nail heads with zinc-phosphate primer.

Before you paint plasterboard with oil paint, prime it with one coat of general-purpose primer. One coat of thinned emulsion may be needed on an absorbent board before the normal full-strength coats are applied.

Prior to hanging wallcovering, seal plasterboard with a general-purpose primer thinned with white spirit. After 48 hours, apply a coat of size. This allows wet-stripping without disturbing the board's paper facing.

Painted plaster

Wash sound paintwork with a sugar-soap or detergent solution. Use water and medium-grade wet-and-dry abrasive paper to key the surface of gloss paint, particularly if covering with emulsion. Prime and allow to dry.

If the ceiling is severely stained by smoke and nicotine, prime it with an alkali-resistant primer or an aluminium spirit-based sealer. Sealers are sold in aerosol cans for treating isolated stains.

If you want to hang wallcovering on oil paint, key then size the wall. Cross-line the wall with lining paper before hanging a heavy embossed paper.

Remove flaking materials with a scraper or stiff-bristle brush. Feather off the edges of the paintwork with wet-and-dry abrasive paper. Treat bare plaster patches with a general-purpose primer. If the edges of old paintwork continue to show, prime those areas again, rubbing down afterwards. Apply stabilizing primer if the paint is friable.

Apply tiles over sound paintwork after removing any loose material.

Cracks in solid plaster

Special flexible emulsions and textured paints are designed to cover hairline cracks, but larger ones will reappear in a relatively short time if they are not filled adequately.

Rake loose material from a crack with the blade of a scraper or filling knife (1). Undercut the edges of larger cracks in order to provide a key for the filling. Mix up interior-grade cellulose filler to a stiff consistency or use a pre-mixed filler.

Dampen the crack with a paintbrush, then press the filler in with a filling knife. Drag the blade across the crack to force the filler in, then draw it along the crack (2) to smooth the filler. Leave the filler standing slightly proud of the surface ready for rubbing down smooth and flush with abrasive paper.

Fill shallow cracks with one application but build up the filler in stages in deep ones, letting each application set before adding more.

Cracks sometimes appear in the corner between walls or a wall and ceiling; fill these by running your finger dipped in filler along the crack. When the filler has hardened, rub it down with medium-grade abrasive paper.

Fill and rub down small holes and dents in solid plasterwork in the same way as for filling cracks.

1 Rake out loose material

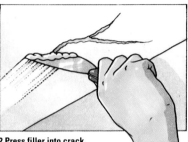

2 Press filler into crack

Large gaps can open up between skirting boards and the wall plaster. Cellulose filler simply falls into the cavity behind, so bridge the gap with a roll of press-in-place butyl sealant.

PATCHING HOLES IN PLASTER

A lath-and-plaster wall

If the laths are intact, plaster up the holes as for solid plasterwork. A hole under 75mm (3in) wide can simply be packed out with a ball of wet newspaper dipped in plaster. Fill flush to the surface with cellulose filler.

If some laths are broken, reinforce the repair with a piece of fine expanded-metal mesh. Rake out loose plaster and undercut the edge of the hole with a bolster chisel. Use tinsnips to cut the metal to the shape of the hole, but a little larger (**1**). The mesh is flexible, so you can easily bend it in order to tuck the edge behind the sound plaster all round (**2**). Flatten it against the laths with light taps from a hammer and, if possible, staple the mesh to a wall stud to hold it (**3**).

Gently apply one thin coat of backing plaster (**4**) and let it dry for about one hour before you continue patching.

1 Cut with tinsnips   **2 Tuck mesh into hole**   **3 Staple mesh to stud**   **4 Trowel on plaster**

A plasterboard wall or ceiling

A large hole punched through a plasterboard wall or ceiling cannot be patched with wet plaster only. Cut back the damaged board to the nearest studs or joists at each side (**1**), using a sharp trimming knife against a straightedge. Cut a new panel of plasterboard to fit snugly within the hole and nail it to the joists or studs using galvanized plasterboard nails. Use a steel trowel to spread finish plaster over the panel, forcing it well into the edges (**2**). Allow the plaster to stiffen, then smooth it with a dry trowel. You may have to add another layer to bring the patch to the level of the wall or ceiling.

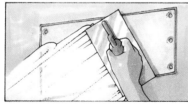

1 Cut damaged panel to nearest supports   **2 Nail on the new panel and coat with plaster**

A small hole in plasterboard

For very small holes in plasterboard use cellulose filler instead of plaster. Use plasterer's glass-fibre patching tape for holes up to about 90mm (3½in) across. Stick on the self-adhesive strips in a star shape over the hole, then apply filler and feather the edges (**1**).

Alternatively, use an offcut of plasterboard just larger than the hole yet narrow enough to slot through. Bore a hole in the middle and thread a length of string through. Tie a galvanized nail to one end of the string (**2**). Butter the ends of the offcut with filler, then feed it into the hole. Pull on the string (**3**) to force it against the back of the cladding, then press filler into the hole so that it is not quite flush with the surface. When the filler is hard, cut off the string and apply a thin coat of filler for a flush finish.

1 Fill and feather the patch   **2 Fix string to offcut**   **3 Pull on string**

DEALING WITH DISTEMPER

Distemper was once a popular finish, so you may have to deal with it if your house is old. It is basically powdered chalk or whiting, mixed with glue size and water. It makes a poor base for decorating: when wet it redissolves and comes away from the surface along with the new decorations.

Brush away all loose material and apply a stabilizing primer to bind any traces left on the surface.

Many delicate plaster mouldings have been obliterated over time with successive coats of distemper. As it is water-soluble, you can remove it with care and patience. Work on a small area at a time, wetting it through with water. Remove the distemper with a toothbrush until the detail of the moulding is clear, then scrape out the softened paint with pointed sticks such as wooden skewers. Wash the moulding and apply a stabilizing primer.

Alternatively, hire a specialist to strip distemper with steam.

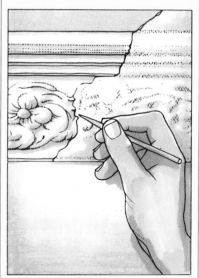

Removing distemper
Scrub with a toothbrush, then scrape out the softened paint with a pointed stick.

Limewash and cement paints

Other water-thinned paints such as limewash and cement paints are less likely to cause problems when you need to overpaint them unless they are in poor condition. Scrape and brush down with a stiff-bristle brush, then wipe the surface with white spirit to remove grease (it is best not to use water on these paints). Ensure the surface is sound by applying a stabilizing primer.

External corners
Dampen the chipped corner, then use a filling knife to scrape the filler on to the damaged edge, working from both sides of the angle (**1**). Let the filler stiffen, then shape it with a wet finger so it closely resembles the original profile (**2**).

1 Use filler knife

2 Shape with finger

● **Lath-and-plaster ceiling**
If the laths are sound, plaster over as for solid plasterwork. If the laths are broken, cut back to the nearest joist and secure with galvanized nails. Fit a panel of plasterboard and spread on a coat of bonding plaster followed by a coat of finish plaster.

PREPARING
WALLCOVERINGS

2 Steam stripper
You can hire a large industrial model or buy a lightweight steam stripper with its own built-in reservoir. Hold the sole plate against the wall until the steam penetrates and softens the paper, then remove it with a scraper. Wash the wall to remove traces of paste.

ERADICATING MOULD GROWTH

If damp conditions are present mould can develop, usually in the form of black specks. The cause of the damp must be remedied before you begin to treat the walls or ceiling.

Sterilize the mould growth before you carry out any other preparatory work to avoid distributing spores into the atmosphere. Apply a liberal wash of a solution made from 1 part household bleach : 16 parts water. (Do not make the solution any stronger as it may damage the wall decoration.) Leave the solution for at least four hours, then carefully scrape off the mould, wipe it on to newspaper and burn it outside.

Wash the wall again with the solution, then leave it for three days in order to sterilize the wall completely. When the wall is dry, paint it with a stabilizing primer thinned with white spirit. If you plan to hang wallpaper, size the wall using a size containing a fungicide solution.

Where mould growth is affecting wallpaper, soak the area in a warm water-and-bleach solution, then scrape off the contaminated paper and burn it. Wash the wall with a fresh bleach solution to remove paste residue.

Apply a liberal wash of similar solution to sterilize the wall and leave it for at least three days, but preferably one week, to make sure no further growth occurs. When the wall is completely dry, apply a stabilizing primer thinned with white spirit, followed by a coat of size if you plan to repaper the wall.

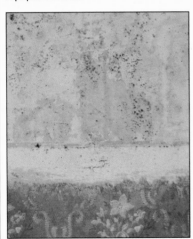

Mould growth
Mould, typified by black specks, will grow on damp plaster or paper.

When you are faced with a previously papered surface the best solution is to strip it completely before hanging new wallcovering. However, if the paper is perfectly sound, you can paint it with emulsion or oil paints (but be warned: it will be more difficult to remove in the future). If the paper has strong reds, greens or blues or metallic inks in the pattern these may show through the paint; mask them by applying an aluminium spirit-based sealer. Do not paint vinyl wallcovering, except for blown vinyl. If you opt for stripping off the old covering, the method you use will depend on the material and how it has been treated.

Stripping wallpaper

Soak the paper with warm water with a little washing-up liquid or proprietary stripping powder or liquid added to soften the adhesive. Apply the water with a sponge or houseplant sprayer. Repeat and leave the water to penetrate for 15 to 20 minutes.

Use a wide metal-bladed scraper to lift the softened paper, starting at the seams. Take care not to dig the points of the blade into the plaster. Resoak stubborn areas of paper and leave them for a few minutes before stripping. Electricity and water are a lethal combination: where possible, dry-strip around switches and sockets. If the paper cannot be stripped dry, switch off the power at the consumer unit when you come to strip around electrical fittings. Unscrew the faceplates so that you can get at the paper trapped behind. Do not use a sprayer near electrical accessories.

Collect all the stripped paper in plastic sacks, then wash the wall with warm water containing a little detergent. From then on, treat the wall as for plaster.

Scoring washable wallpaper

Washable wallpaper has an impervious surface film, which you must break through to allow the water to penetrate to the adhesive.

Use a toothed perforating wheel, a wire brush or a serrated scraper to score the surface, then soak it with warm water and stripper. It may take several applications of the liquid before the paper begins to lift.

Peeling off vinyl wallcovering

Vinyl wallcovering consists of a thin layer of vinyl fused with a paper backing. It is possible to peel off the vinyl, leaving the backing paper on the wall; the latter can then be either painted or used as a lining for a new wallcovering.

To remove the vinyl, lift both bottom corners of the top layer of the wallcovering, then pull firmly and steadily away from the wall. Either soak and scrape off the backing paper or, if you want to leave it as a lining paper, smooth the seams with medium-grade abrasive paper, using very light pressure to avoid wearing a hole.

Stripping painted wallcoverings

Wallcoverings which have been painted can be difficult to remove. If the paper is sound, simply prepare it in the same way as painted plaster and decorate over it.

To strip it, use a wire brush or home-made scraper (**1**) to score the surface, then soak with warm water plus a little paper stripper. Painted papers (and washables) can easily be stripped using a steam stripper. Hold the stripper plate against the paper until the steam penetrates, then remove the soaked paper with a wide-bladed scraper (**2**).

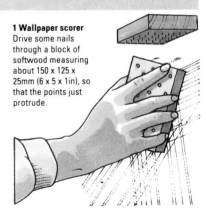

1 Wallpaper scorer
Drive some nails through a block of softwood measuring about 150 x 125 x 25mm (6 x 5 x 1in), so that the points just protrude.

A sanded wooden floor sealed with a clear finish that highlights its grain is a most attractive feature for many rooms. Although straightforward, the job is laborious, dusty and extremely noisy. Considerable patience is also required in order to achieve an even, scratch-free and long-lasting finish.

Repairing the floorboards

There is no point in spending time and money sanding floorboards which are in poor condition, so examine them first. Look for any boards with signs of woodworm infestation. If the beetle is still active, treat the remaining boards and joists below with a proprietary woodworm fluid. Even if the beetle has been eradicated, replace any boards that have more than a few holes in them: beneath the surface there may well be a honeycomb of tunnels made by the woodworm larvae. As the process of sanding will remove a lot of timber, these tunnels may be revealed on the surface of the boards.

If you find signs of dry or wet rot when you lift up a floorboard, have it treated straightaway before you make a start on the sanding.

Examine the floor for boards which have been lifted previously by

electricians and plumbers. Replace any that are split, too short or badly jointed. Try to find second-hand boards to match the rest of the floor, but if you have to use new wood, stain or bleach it after the floor has been sanded to match the colour of the old boards. Drive all nail heads below the surface with a punch and hammer: a raised head will rip the abrasive paper on the sander's drum.

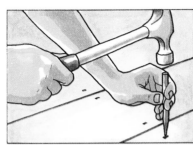

Sink nail heads below the surface

Filling gaps between the floorboards

What you do about gaps between boards depends on how much they bother you. Many people simply ignore them, but you will end up with a superior job as well as improved draughtproofing if you make the effort to fill them invisibly or close them up.

Closing up
Over a large area, the quickest and most satisfactory solution is to lift the boards a few at a time and re-lay them butted side by side, filling in the final gap with a new board.

Filling with papier mâché
If there are a few gaps only, make up a stiff papier-mâché paste with white newsprint and wallpaper paste, plus a

little water-based wood dye to colour it to match the sanded floor. Scrape out dirt and wax from between the boards and press the paste into the gap with a filling knife. Press it well below the level likely to be reached by the sander and fill flush with the floor surface. Run the blade along the gap to smooth it.

Inserting a wooden lath
Large gaps can be filled by a thin wooden lath planed to fit tightly between the boards. Apply a little PVA adhesive to the gap and tap the lath in with a hammer until it is flush with the surface. Skim with a plane if necessary. Do not bother to fill several gaps this way: it is easier to close up the boards and fill one gap with a new floorboard.

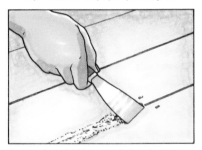

Force papier mâché between the boards

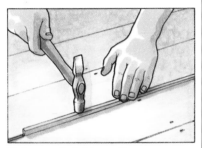

Wedge a wooden lath into a wide gap

CHOOSING A SANDING MACHINE

The area of a floor is far too large to contemplate sanding with anything but an industrial sanding machine. You can obtain such equipment from the usual tool-hire outlets, which also supply the abrasive papers. You will need three grades of paper: coarse, to level the boards initially, followed by medium and fine to achieve a smooth finish.

It is best to hire a large upright drum sander for the main floor area and a smaller rotary sander for tackling the edges. You can use the rotary sander only for smaller rooms such as bathrooms and WCs.

Some companies also supply a scraper for cleaning out inaccessible corners, but do make sure it is fitted with a new blade when you hire it.

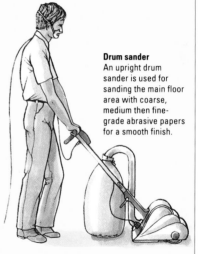

Drum sander
An upright drum sander is used for sanding the main floor area with coarse, medium then fine-grade abrasive papers for a smooth finish.

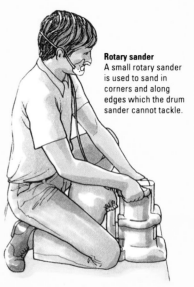

Rotary sander
A small rotary sander is used to sand in corners and along edges which the drum sander cannot tackle.

Hook scraper
Use a small hook scraper for removing paint spots from the floor, and for reaching into spaces that are inaccessible to the rotary sander. The tool cuts on the backward stroke; various sizes and blade shapes are available to deal with most situations.

USING SANDING MACHINES

Fitting the abrasive sheet

Precise instructions for fitting abrasive paper to sanding machines should be included with the hired kit. If they are not, ask the hirer to demonstrate what you need to do. Never attempt to change abrasive papers while a machine is plugged into a socket.

With most machines the paper is wrapped round the drum and secured with a screw-down bar (1). Ensure that the paper is wrapped tightly around the drum: if it is slack it may slip from its clamp and will be torn to pieces.

Rotary sanders take a disc of abrasive, usually clamped to the sole plate by a central nut (2).

1 Drum sander   **2 Rotary sander**

Operating a drum sander

Stand at the beginning of a run with the drum sander tilted back so that the drum itself is clear of the floor. Drape the electric lead over one shoulder to make sure it cannot become caught in the sander.

Switch on the machine, then gently lower the drum on to the floor. There is no need to push a drum sander: it will move forward under its own power. Hold the machine in check so that it proceeds at a slow but steady walking place along a straight line. Do not hold it still for even a brief period as it will rapidly sand a deep hollow in the floorboards. Take care you do not let go of it, either, as it will run across the room on its own, probably damaging the floorboards in the process.

When you reach the other side of the room tilt the machine back, switch off and wait for it to stop before lowering it to the floor.

If the abrasive paper rips, tilt the machine on to its back castors and switch off. Wait for the drum to stop revolving, disconnect the power, then change the paper.

Sanding cleans and rejuvenates wooden floors

Using a rotary sander

Hold the handles on top of the machine and drape the flex over your shoulder. Tilt the sander on to its back castors to lift the disc off the floor. Switch on and lower the machine. As soon as you contact the boards, sweep the machine in any direction, but keep it moving. As soon as it comes to rest the disc will score deep, scorched swirl marks in the wood which are difficult to remove. There is no need to press down on the machine. When you have finished, tilt back the machine and switch off, leaving the motor to run down.

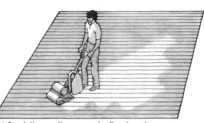

1 Sand diagonally across the floorboards

Sanding procedure

A great deal of dust is produced by sanding a floor, so before you begin empty the room of furniture and take down curtains, lampshades and pictures. Seal around the room door with masking tape and stuff folded newspaper under it. Open all windows. Wear old clothes and a dust mask.

Sweep the floor to remove grit and other debris. Old floorboards will most likely be curved across their width (cupped), so the first task is to level the floor across its entire area.

With coarse paper fitted in the drum sander, sand diagonally across the room (1). At the end of the run, tilt the machine, pull it back and make a second run parallel to the first. Allow each pass to overlap the last slightly.

When you have covered the floor once, sand it again in the same way, but this time across the opposite diagonal of the room (2). Sweep the sawdust from the floor after each run is completed.

Once the floor is flat and clean all over, change to a medium-grade paper and sand parallel to the boards (3). Overlap each pass as before. Finally, switch to the fine-grade paper in order to remove all obvious scratches and give a smooth finish, working parallel to the boards and overlapping each pass again. Each time you change the grade of paper on the drum sander, put the same grade on the rotary sander and sand the edges of the room so that they are finished to the same standard as the main area (4).

Even the rotary sander cannot clean right up to the skirting or into the corners; finish these small areas with a scraper, or fit a flexible abrasive disc in a power drill.

Vacuum the floor and wipe it over with a cloth dampened with white spirit ready for finishing.

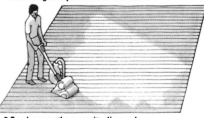

2 Sand across the opposite diagonal

3 Sand parallel to the floorboards

4 Finish the edges with the rotary sander

The wooden joinery in our homes needs redecorating long before any other part of the house, particularly bargeboards and fascias and the exterior of windows and doors. The cause is in the nature of the wood itself, which swells when it becomes moist, then shrinks again when the sun or central heating dries it out. Paint will not adhere for long under these conditions, nor will any other finish. Wood is also vulnerable to woodworm and various forms of rot caused primarily by damp, so careful preparation is essential to preserve most types of timber.

Treating new timber

A lot of new joinery is primed at the factory, but check that the primer is in good condition before you begin work: it may be quite some time since the timber was delivered from the factory. If the primer is satisfactory, rub it down lightly with fine-grade abrasive paper, dust it off, then apply a second coat of wood primer to areas that will be inaccessible after installation. Do not leave the timber uncovered outside, as primer is not sufficient protection against prolonged exposure to the weather.

To prepare bare timber, make sure it is dry, then sand the surface in the direction of the grain, using a fine-grade glasspaper (wrap it round a wood block for flat surfaces and a piece of dowel or a pencil for moulded sections).

Once you have removed all raised grain and lightly rounded any sharp edges, dust the wood down. Finally, rub it over with a tack rag (an impregnated cloth to which dust will stick) or with a rag moistened with white spirit.

Seal resinous knots with shellac knotting

Knots and other resinous areas of the wood must be treated to prevent them staining subsequent paint layers. Pick off any hardened resin, then seal the knots by painting them with two coats of shellac knotting if you plan to paint with pale finishing colours; if you will be using darker paints, seal the knots and prime the timber in one operation with aluminium primer.

Alternatively, paint bare softwood with a solvent-based wood primer or a quick-drying water-thinned acrylic primer. Apply either primer liberally, taking care to work it well into the joints

and particularly the end grain (which will require at least two coats to give it adequate protection).

Wash oily hardwoods with white spirit immediately prior to priming with an aluminium primer. Use standard wood primers for other hardwoods, thinning them slightly to encourage penetration into the grain.

When the primer is dry, fill open-grained timber with a fine surface filler. Use a piece of coarse cloth to rub it well into the wood, making circular strokes followed by parallel strokes in the direction of the grain. When the filler is dry, rub it down with a fine abrasive paper to a smooth finish.

Fill larger holes, open joints, cracks and similar imperfections with flexible interior or exterior wood filler. Press the filler into the holes with a filling knife, leaving it slightly proud of the surface so that it can be sanded flush with fine-grade abrasive paper once it has set. Dust down ready for painting. If you find a hole you have missed just before you start applying the undercoat, fill it with putty; unlike other fillers, you can paint straight over putty without having to wait for it to dry, although you should wait until it forms a skin.

Using grain filler

If you plan to clear-finish an open-grained timber, apply a proprietary grain filler after sanding. Use a natural filler for pale timbers: for darker wood, buy a filler that matches the timber. Rub the filler across the grain with a coarse rag, leave to harden for several hours, then rub off the excess along the grain with a clean coarse rag.

Apply grain filler with a coarse rag

Preparing for a clear finish

There is no need to apply knotting when you intend to finish the timber with a clear varnish or lacquer. Sand the wood in the direction of the grain using progressively finer grades of abrasive paper, then seal it with a slightly thinned coat of the intended finish.

If the wood is in contact with the ground or in proximity to previous outbreaks of dry rot, treat it first with a liberal wash of clear timber preserver. Check with the manufacturer's recommendations that the liquid is compatible with the finish.

Cellulose filler would show through a clear finish, so use a proprietary stopper to fill imperfections: these are thick pastes made in a range of colours to suit the type of timber. You can adjust the colour further by mixing the stopper with wood dyes. As stoppers can be oil-based or water-based, make sure you use a similar-based dye. Where possible, use an oil-based stopper outside. Fill the blemishes as before and rub down when the stopper hardens.

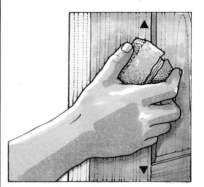

Sand along the grain with abrasive paper

PAINTED AND VARNISHED WOODWORK

Most of the joinery in and around your house will have been painted or varnished at some time and provided it is in good condition it will form a sound base for new paintwork. However, when too many coats of paint have been applied, the mouldings around doorframes and window frames begin to look poorly defined and the paintwork has a lumpy and unattractive appearance. In such a case it is best to strip off all the old paint down to bare wood and start again. Stripping is also essential where the paintwork has deteriorated and is blistering, crazing or flaking.

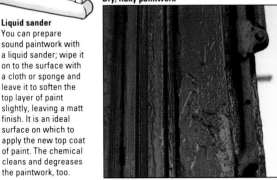

Dry, flaky paintwork

Liquid sander
You can prepare sound paintwork with a liquid sander; wipe it on to the surface with a cloth or sponge and leave it to soften the top layer of paint slightly, leaving a matt finish. It is an ideal surface on which to apply the new top coat of paint. The chemical cleans and degreases the paintwork, too.

● **Flexible acrylic filler**
An acrylic filler is ideal for filling large cracks or gaps in painted woodwork. It is squeezed into the gap from a cartridge gun and smoothed with a damp cloth — no sanding is required. You can overpaint one hour later.

Heavily overpainted woodwork

Badly weathered varnish

Preparing sound paintwork

Wash the paintwork from the bottom upwards with a solution of warm water and sugar soap or detergent. Pay particular attention to the areas around the door handles and window catches, where dirt and grease will be heaviest. Rinse with fresh water from bottom to top to prevent runs of dirty liquid staining the surface.

Rub down gloss paintwork with fine-grade wet-and-dry abrasive paper dipped in water in order to provide a key for the new finish coat and to remove any blemishes. Prime bare patches of wood. Build up these low spots gradually with undercoat, rubbing down between each application.

Fill open joints or holes with filler and rub down when set. Renew crumbling putty and seal around window frames and doorframes with mastic, then proceed with undercoat and top coat.

Preparing unsound paintwork or varnish

Unsound paintwork or varnish such as the examples pictured left must be stripped to bare wood. There are several methods you can use, but always scrape off loose material first.

In some cases, where the paint is particularly dry and flaky, dry-scraping may be all that is required, using a proprietary hook scraper and finishing with a light rub down with abrasive paper. Where most of the paint is stuck firmly to the woodwork, remove it using one of the methods described below and on the facing page.

Stripping paint and varnish with a blowtorch

The traditional method for stripping old paint is to burn it off with a blowtorch fuelled with liquid gas from a pressurized canister, but you can also obtain more sophisticated blowtorches that are connected by a hose to a metal gas bottle of the type used for camping or in caravans. This type of gas torch is finely adjustable, so is useful for other jobs such as brazing and soldering.

To reduce the risk of fire, take down curtains and pelmets and, outside, rake out old birds' nests from behind your roof fascia board and soffit.

It is only necessary to soften the paint with a flame to scrape it off, but it is all too easy to heat the paint so that it is actually burning. Deposit scrapings in a metal paint kettle or bucket as you remove them.

Start by stripping mouldings from the bottom upwards. Never direct the flame at one spot but keep it moving all the time so that you do not scorch the wood. As soon as the paint has softened, use a shavehook to scrape it off. If it is sticky or hard, heat it a little more then try scraping again.

Having dealt with the mouldings, strip flat areas of woodwork, using a wide-bladed stripping knife. When you have finished stripping, sand the wood with medium-grade abrasive paper to remove hardened specks of paint and any accidental light scorching.

It may prove impossible to sand away heavy scorching without removing too much wood. Sand or scrape off loose blackened wood fibres, fill any hollows and repaint the woodwork, having primed the scorched areas with an aluminium wood primer.

Shavehook, used for mouldings

Scraper, used for flat surfaces

SELECTING AND USING CHEMICAL STRIPPERS

An old finish can be removed using a stripper that reacts chemically with paint or varnish. There are general-purpose strippers that will soften both solvent-based and water-based finishes, including emulsions and cellulose paints, as well as strippers that are formulated to react with a specific type of finish such as textured paint or varnish. Dedicated strippers achieve the desired result more efficiently than general-purpose ones, but at the cost of you having to acquire a whole range of specialist products.

Traditionally, strippers have been manufactured from highly potent chemicals that have to be handled with care. Working with this type of stripper means having to wear protective gloves and safety glasses, and possibly a respirator too. The newer generation of so-called 'green' strippers do not burn your skin nor do they exude harmful fumes. However, removing paint with these milder strippers is a relatively slow process. Whichever type of stripper you decide to use, always follow the manufacturer's health-and-safety recommendations and if in doubt err on the side of caution.

Before you opt for a particular stripper, you should also consider the nature of the surface you intend to strip. The thick, gel-like paint removers that will cling to vertical surfaces such as doors and wall panelling are perfect for all general household joinery. Strippers made to a thinner consistency are perhaps best employed on delicately carved work. For good-quality furniture, especially if it is veneered, make sure you use a stripper that can be washed off with white spirit as water will raise the grain and may soften old glue.

Working with chemical strippers

Lay polyethylene sheets or plenty of newspaper on the floor, then apply a liberal coat of stripper to the paintwork, stippling it well into any mouldings. Leave it for 10 to 20 minutes, then try scraping a patch to see if the paint has softened through to the wood. (You might have to leave one of the milder strippers in contact with the paint for 45 minutes or longer.) Do not waste your time removing the top coats of paint only, but apply more stripper and stipple the partially softened finish back down with a brush so the stripper will soak through to the wood. Leave it for another 5 to 10 minutes.

Once the chemicals have completed their work, use a stripping knife to scrape paint from flat surfaces and a shavehook to remove it from mouldings.

Wipe the paint from deep carvings with fine wire wool, except when stripping oak; use small pieces of coarse sacking for the latter as particles of metal can stain the wood.

Having removed the bulk of the paint, clean off residual patches with a wad of wire wool dipped in fresh stripper. Rub with the grain, turning the wad inside out to present a clean face as it becomes clogged with paint. Neutralize the stripper by washing the wood with white spirit or water, depending on the manufacturer's advice.

Let the wood dry out thoroughly, then prepare it as if it were new timber.

Industrial stripping

Any portable woodwork can be taken to a professional stripper, who will immerse the whole thing in a tank of stripping solution of hot caustic soda which must then be washed out of the wood by hosing down with water. It is an efficient process (which incidentally kills woodworm at the same time), but it risks splitting panels, warping the wood and opening up joints. At best, you can expect a reasonable amount of raised grain, which you will have to sand before refinishing.

Some companies use a cold chemical dip, which does little harm to solid timber and raises the grain less. However, this treatment is likely to prove more expensive than the caustic-soda process.

Most stripping companies will collect; many will rehang a door for you, and some offer a finishing service, too.

Never submit veneered items to industrial treatment: veneers were formerly applied with animal glues, which may be dissolved by the chemical so that the veneer peels off. Instead, strip the items with a chemical stripper and finish off by wiping them with white spirit.

Using a hot-air stripper

Although stripping paint with a flame is fast and efficient, there is always the risk that you will burn the wood. Scorching can be covered with paint, but if you want to varnish the stripped wood scorch marks will mar the finish.

Electrically-heated guns – like powerful hair dryers – work almost as quickly as a blowtorch but with less risk of scorching or fire. They operate at an extremely high temperature: under no circumstances test the stripper by holding your hand over the nozzle.

Some guns come with variable heat settings and a selection of nozzles for various uses (see below). Hold the gun about 50mm (2in) from the surface of the paintwork and move it slowly backwards and forwards until the paint blisters and bubbles. Immediately remove the paint with a shavehook or scraper. Aim to heat the paint just ahead of the scraper so you develop a continuous work action.

Fit a shaped nozzle on to the gun when stripping glazing bars to deflect the jet of hot air and reduce the risk of cracking the glass.

Old primer can sometimes be difficult to remove with a hot-air stripper. This is not a problem if you are repainting the timber; just rub the surface down with abrasive paper. For a clear finish, remove residues of paint from the grain with wads of wire wool dipped in chemical stripper (see left).

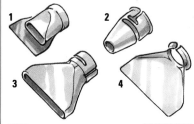

With a hot-air gun there is less risk of scorching

PAINTED AND
VARNISHED
WOODWORK

SEE ALSO

Details for:	
Primers	21
Preparing timber	27
Finishing wood	36–46

Nozzles for hot-air guns
Hot-air strippers come with a standard wide mouth for general usage. Most manufacturers offer optional extras, typically a push-on nozzle with an integral scraper (**1**), a conical nozzle to concentrate the heat on a small area (**2**), a flared nozzle to spread the heat (**3**) and a nozzle that protects the glass when you strip glazing bars (**4**).

29

Metals are used extensively for window frames, railings, gutters, pipework, radiators and door furniture in both modern and period homes. Areas of metal that are exposed to the elements, or are in close proximity to water, are usually prone to corrosion. Many paints on their own do not afford sufficient protection against corrosion, so special treatments and coatings are often required to prolong the life of the metal.

Cast-iron railings deeply pitted with rust

Flaking casement window as a result of rust

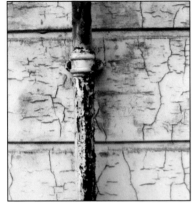
Severely corroded cast-iron drainpipe

What is rust?

Rust is a form of corrosion that affects ferrous metals – notably iron and steel – due to the combination of water, oxygen and carbon dioxide. Although most paints slow down the rate at which moisture penetrates, they do not bar it altogether; primers are needed to complete the protection, and the type you use depends on the condition of the metal and how you plan to decorate it. Make your preparation thorough or the job will be ruined.

Treating bare metal

Remove light deposits of rust by rubbing with wire wool or wet-and-dry abrasive paper dipped in white spirit. If the rust is heavy and the surface of the metal pitted, use a wire brush or, for extensive corrosion, a wire wheel or cup brush in a power drill. Wear goggles while wire-brushing in order to protect your eyes from flying particles.

Use a zinc-phosphate primer to protect metal inside the house. You can use the same primer outdoors, too, but if you are painting previously rusted metal, especially if it is in a very exposed location, use a high-performance rust-inhibitive primer.

Work primers into crevices and fixings, and make sure sharp edges and corners where corrosion often begins are coated generously.

Preparing previously painted metal

If the paint is perfectly sound wash it with sugar soap or a detergent solution, then rinse and dry it. Rub down gloss paint with fine wet-and-dry abrasive paper to provide a key.

If the paint film is blistered or flaking where water has penetrated and corrosion has set in, remove all loose paint and rust with a wire brush or a wire wheel or cup brush in a power drill. Apply rust-inhibitive primer to bare patches, working it well into joints, bolt heads and other fixings. Prime bare metal immediately as rust can re-form very rapidly.

When you are preparing cast-iron guttering, brush out dead leaves and other debris and wash it clean. Coat the inside with a bitumen paint. If you want to paint over old bitumen paint, use an aluminium primer first to prevent it bleeding to the surface.

Stripping painted metal

Delicately moulded sections – on fire surrounds, garden furniture and other cast or wrought ironwork – will often benefit from stripping off old paint and rust which is masking fine detail. They cannot easily be rubbed down with a wire brush and a hot-air stripper cannot be used here as the metal dissipates the heat before the paint softens. A gas blowtorch can be used to strip wrought ironwork, but cast iron might crack if it becomes distorted by localized heating.

Chemical stripping is the safest method, but before you begin check that what appears to be a metal fire surround is not in fact made from plaster mouldings on a wooden background: the stripping process can play havoc with soft plasterwork. Tap the surround to see if it is metallic, or scrape an inconspicuous section.

Paint the bare metal with a rust-inhibitive primer or, alternatively, a proprietary rust-killing jelly or liquid which will remove and neutralize rust: usually based on phosphoric acid, they combine with the rust to leave it quite inert in the form of iron phosphate. Some rust killers will deal with minute particles invisible to the naked eye and are self-priming so that no additional primer is required.

Alternatively, if the metalwork is portable, you can take it to a sandblaster or an industrial stripper. None of the disadvantages of industrial stripping apply to metal.

Clean the stripped metal with a wire brush, then wash it with white spirit before applying a finish.

In decorating terms, a finish means a liquid or semi-liquid substance which sets, dries or cures to protect and sometimes colour materials such as wood or masonry. Apart from paint, other finishes for wood include stains, varnishes, oil, wax and French polish, all of which are used specifically where you want to display the grain of the timber for its natural beauty.

The make-up of paint

Paint is made from solid particles of pigment suspended in a liquid binder or medium. The pigment provides the colour and body of the paint, while the medium allows the material to be brushed, rolled or sprayed and, once applied, forms a solid film binding the pigment together and adhering to the surface. Binder and pigment vary from paint to paint, but the two most common types are solvent-based (sometimes known as oil-based) and water-based.

COMMON PAINT FINISHES AND ADDITIVES

The type of paint you choose depends on the finish you want and the material you are decorating. Various additives adapt the paint's qualities.

Solvent-based (oil) paints

The medium for solvent-based paints (commonly called oil paints) is a mixture of oils and resin. A paint made from a natural resin is slow-drying, but modern paints contain a synthetic resin such as alkyd, which makes for a faster-drying finish. Various pigments determine the colour of the paint.

Water-based paints

Emulsion is perhaps the most familiar type of water-based paint. It, too, is manufactured with a synthetic resin, usually vinyl, which is dispersed in a solution of water. Water-based acrylic paints are primarily intended for finishing interior or exterior woodwork. They tend to dry with a semi-matt sheen rather than a full gloss.

Additives in paint

No paint is made simply from binder and pigment; certain additives are included during manufacture to give the paint qualities such as faster drying time, high gloss, easy flow or longer pot life, or to make it non-drip.
● **Thixotropic** paints are the typical non-drip types; they are thick, almost jelly-like in the can, enabling you to pick up a brushload without it dripping.
● **Extenders** are added as fillers to strengthen the paint film. Cheap paint contains too much filler, reducing its covering power.

Paint thinners

If a paint is too thick it cannot be applied properly and must be thinned before it is used. Some finishes, such as low-odour paints, require special thinners provided by the manufacturer, but most oil paints can be thinned with white spirit, and emulsions with water. Turpentine will thin oil paint, but has no advantages over white spirit for household paints and is much more expensive.

Gloss or matt finish?

The proportion of pigment to resin affects the way the paint sets. A gloss (shiny) paint contains approximately equal amounts of resin and pigment, whereas a higher proportion of pigment produces a matt (dull) paint. By adjusting the proportions, it is possible to make satin or eggshell paints. Matt paints tend to cover best due to their high pigment content, while the greater proportion of resin in gloss paints is responsible for their strength.

Applying a paint system

Unless you are using one of the specially formulated one-coat finishes, it is necessary to apply successive layers to build up a paint system.

● Painting walls requires a simple system, comprising two or three coats of the same paint.
● Painting woodwork and metalwork usually involves a more complex system, using paints with different qualities. A typical paint system for woodwork is illustrated below.

SEE ALSO

Details for:	
Choosing colours	6-7
Lead content	21
Primers	21
Preparing paint	32

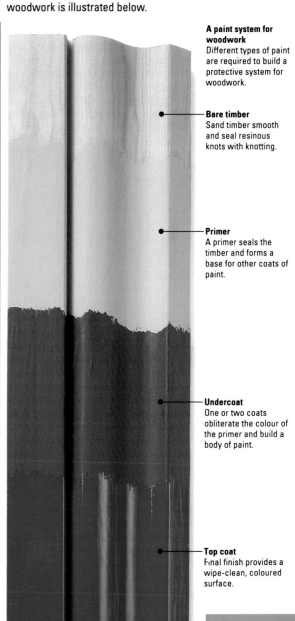

A paint system for woodwork
Different types of paint are required to build a protective system for woodwork.

Bare timber
Sand timber smooth and seal resinous knots with knotting.

Primer
A primer seals the timber and forms a base for other coats of paint.

Undercoat
One or two coats obliterate the colour of the primer and build a body of paint.

Top coat
Final finish provides a wipe-clean, coloured surface.

31

PAINTING
EXTERIOR
MASONRY

SEE ALSO
Details for:
Ladders and towers   18-20

SAFETY WHEN PAINTING

DECORATING WITH SOLVENT-BASED PAINT IS NOT DANGEROUS PROVIDED YOU TAKE SENSIBLE PRECAUTIONS.

● Ensure good ventilation indoors while applying a finish and when it is drying. Wear a respirator if you suffer from breathing disorders.
● Do not smoke while painting or in the vicinity of drying paint.
● Contain paint spillages outside with sand or earth and don't allow any paint to enter a drain.
● If you splash paint in your eyes, flush them with copious amounts of water with your lids held open; if symptoms persist, visit a doctor.
● Always wear barrier cream or gloves if you have sensitive skin. Use a proprietary skin cleaner to remove paint from your skin or wash it off with warm soapy water. Do not use paint thinners to clean your skin.
● Keep any finish and thinners out of reach of children. If a child swallows a substance, do not make any attempt to induce him or her to vomit – seek medical treatment instead.

Strain old paint
If you're using leftover paint, filter it through a piece of muslin or old tights stretched over the rim of a container.

Resealing the lid
Wipe the rim of the can clean before you replace the lid, then tap it down all round with a hammer over a softwood block.

PREPARING THE PAINT

Whether you're using newly purchased paint or leftovers from previous jobs, there are some basic rules to observe before you apply it.

● Wipe dust from the paint can, then prise off the lid with the side of a knife blade. Don't use a screwdriver: it only buckles the edge of the lid, preventing an airtight seal and making subsequent removal difficult.
● Gently stir liquid paints with a wooden stick to blend the pigment and medium. There's no need to stir thixotropic paints unless the medium has separated; if you have to stir it, leave it to gel again before using.
● If a skin has formed on paint, cut round the edge with a knife and lift out in one piece with a stick. It's a good idea to store the can on its lid, so that a skin cannot form on top of the paint.
● Whether the paint is old or new, transfer a small amount into a paint kettle or plastic bucket. Old paint should be filtered at the same time, tying a piece of muslin or old nylon tights across the rim of the kettle.

The outside walls of houses are painted for two major reasons: to give a clean, bright appearance and to protect the surface from the rigours of the climate. What you use as a finish and how you apply it depends on what the walls are made of, their condition and the degree of protection they need. Bricks are traditionally left bare, but may require a coat of paint if previous attempts to decorate have resulted in a poor finish. Rendered walls are often painted to brighten the naturally dull grey colour of the cement; pebbledashed surfaces may need a colourful coat to disguise previous conspicuous patches. On the other hand, you may just want to change the present colour of your walls for a fresh appearance.

Working to a plan

Before you embark upon painting the outside walls of your house, plan your time carefully. Depending on the amount of preparation that is required, even a small house will take a few weeks to complete.

It is not necessary to tackle the whole job at once – although it is preferable, as the weather may change to the detriment of your timetable. You can split the work into separate stages with days (even weeks) in between, provided you divide the walls into manageable sections. Use window frames and doorframes, bays, downpipes and corners of walls to form break lines that will disguise joins.

Start at the top of the house, working from right to left if you are right-handed and vice versa.

● Black dot denotes compatibility.
All surfaces must be clean, sound, dry and free from organic growth.

FINISHES FOR MASONRY

SUITABLE TO COVER	Cement paint	Water-based masonry paint	Reinforced masonry paint	Solvent-based masonry paint	Textured coating	Floor paint
Brick	●	●	●	●	●	●
Stone	●	●	●	●	●	●
Concrete	●	●	●	●	●	●
Cement rendering	●	●	●	●	●	●
Pebbledash	●	●	●	●	●	●
Emulsion paint		●	●	●	●	●
Solvent-based paint		●	●	●	●	●
Cement paint	●	●	●	●	●	●
DRYING TIME: HOURS						
Touch dry	1–2	1–2	2–3	4–6	6	2–3
Recoatable	24	4–6	24	16	24–48	3–16
THINNERS: SOLVENTS						
Water	●	●	●		●	●
White spirit			●	●		●
NUMBER OF COATS						
Normal conditions	2	2	1–2	2	1	1–2
COVERAGE: DEPENDING ON WALL TEXTURE						
Sq metres per litre		4–10	3–6.5	6–16	2	5–10
Sq metres per kg	1–6				1–2	
METHOD OF APPLICATION						
Brush	●	●	●	●	●	●
Roller	●	●	●	●	●	●
Spray gun	●	●	●	●		

PAINTS
WALLS/CEILINGS

PAINTING
INTERIOR WALLS
AND CEILINGS

SEE ALSO
Details for:
Primers and sealers	21
Preparation	22–23
Stripping wallcoverings	24

Unless the house has been recently built, most of the interior walls and ceilings will be plastered and probably papered or painted too. Preparation varies, but the methods for painting them are identical and they can be considered smooth surfaces in terms of paint coverage. A matt paint is usually preferred, but there's no reason why you shouldn't use a gloss or satin finish.

Finishes for bare masonry

Some interior walls are left unplastered, either for the sake of a decorative appearance or because it is considered unnecessary to clad the walls of certain rooms such as the basement, workshop or garage. Some have been deliberately stripped for effect – a brick or stone chimney breast, for example, acts as an attractive focal point in a room, and an entire wall of bare masonry can make a dramatic impression.

If you want to finish brick, concrete or stone walls, follow the methods described for exterior walls. However, because in this case they do not have to withstand any weathering, you can use paint designed for interiors. Newly stripped masonry will require sealing first with a stabilizing primer in order to bind the surface.

SELECTING PAINTS FOR INTERIOR SURFACES

Emulsion paint is most people's first choice for internal decorations: it is relatively cheap, practically odourless and there are several qualities of paint to suit different circumstances. However, some situations demand a combination of paints to provide the required degree of protection or simply to achieve a pleasing contrast of surface textures.

Emulsion paints

Vinyl emulsions are the most popular and practical paints for walls and ceilings. They are available in liquid or thixotropic consistencies, with matt or satin (semi-gloss) finishes. A satin emulsion is less likely to show fingerprints or scuffs, and non-drip thixotropic paints have obvious advantages when painting ceilings.

One-coat emulsion
You will need to apply two coats of standard emulsion to avoid a patchy, uneven appearance, perhaps thinning the first coat slightly when decorating porous surfaces. A one-coat high-opacity emulsion is intended to save you time, but you will not get satisfactory results if you try to spread the paint too far, especially when overpainting strong colours.

New-plaster emulsion
New-plaster emulsions are specially formulated for new interior walls and ceilings to allow moisture vapour to escape. Standard vinyl emulsions are not sufficiently permeable.

Gloss and satin paints

Paints primarily intended for woodwork can be applied to walls and ceilings that require an extra degree of protection, and similar paints are ideal for decorating the disparate elements of a period-style dado – wooden rail, skirting and embossed wallcovering.

Gloss paints tend to accentuate uneven wall surfaces, so most people prefer a satin (eggshell) finish.

You can use any of the standard spirit-thinned paints on walls and ceilings, but for a faster drying time choose water-based acrylic paints.

Textured paints

Provided the masonry or plaster is basically sound, you can obliterate any unsightly cracks with just one coat of textured paint. A coarse high-build paint will cover cracks up to 2mm (1⁄16in) wide, but there are also fine-texture paints for areas where people may brush against the wall. Available with a matt or satin finish, the paint is normally applied with a coarse-foam roller, but you can use a synthetic-fibre roller if you want to create a finer texture.

Cement paint

Cement paint is an inexpensive exterior finish which is ideal for a utilitarian area indoors, such as a cellar, workshop or garage. Sold in dry-powder form, it must be made up with water and dries to a matt finish.

A painted decorative dado adds character to an old house

Paints for walls and ceilings
Emulsion paint, in its many forms, is the most practical finish for interior walls and ceilings, but use an acrylic or solvent-based paint on wall-fixed joinery like skirtings and picture rails. The example above illustrates the advantage of contrasting textures: matt emulsion for the walls up to the cornice; gloss paint for the dado rail and skirting; satin emulsion for the embossed dado.

USING BRUSHES, PADS AND ROLLERS

Applying paint by brush

Choose a good-quality brush for painting walls and ceilings. Cheap brushes tend to shed bristles, which is both infuriating and less economical in the long run. A brush about 200mm (8in) wide will give the quickest coverage, but if you are not used to handling a brush your wrist will soon tire; you may find a 150mm (6in) brush, plus a 50mm (2in) brush for the edges and corners, more comfortable to use, although the job will take longer.

Loading the brush

Don't overload a brush with paint; it leads to messy work and ruins the bristles if the paint is allowed to dry in the roots. Dip no more than the first third of the brush into the paint, wiping off excess on the side of the container to prevent drips (1). When using thixotropic paint, load the brush and apply paint without removing excess.

Using a brush

You can hold the brush whichever way feels comfortable to you, but the 'pen' grip is the most versatile, enabling your wrist to move the brush freely in any direction. Hold the brush handle between your thumb and forefinger, with your fingers on the ferrule (metal band) and your thumb supporting it from the other side (2).

Apply the paint in vertical strokes, then spread it at right angles to even out the coverage. Emulsion paint will not show brush marks when it dries, but finish oil paints with light upward vertical strokes for the best results.

1 Dip only the first third of bristles in paint

2 Place fingers on ferrule, thumb behind

Applying paint by roller

A paint roller with interchangeable sleeves is an excellent tool for applying paint to large areas. Choose a roller about 225mm (9in) long for painting walls and ceilings. Larger ones are available, but they become tiring to use.

There are a number of different sleeves to suit the type of paint and texture of the surface. Long-haired sheepskin and synthetic-fibre sleeves are excellent on textured surfaces, especially with emulsion paint. Choose a shorter pile for smooth surfaces, and with gloss or satin paints.

Disposable plastic-foam rollers can be used to apply some specialist paints, but they soon lose their resilience and have a tendency to skid across the wall.

Special rollers

Rollers with long detachable extension handles are ideal for painting ceilings without having to erect a work platform.

Narrow rollers for painting behind radiators are invaluable if the radiators cannot be removed from the wall.

Loading a roller

You will need a special paint tray to load a standard roller. Having dipped the sleeve lightly into the paint reservoir, roll it gently onto the ribbed part of the tray to coat the roller evenly (1).

Using a roller

Use zig-zag strokes with a roller (2), painting the surface in all directions to achieve an even coverage. Keep the roller on the surface at all times. If you let it spin at the end of a stroke it will spatter paint onto the floor or adjacent surface. When applying oil paint, finish in one direction, preferably towards prevailing light.

1 Dip roller in paint, roll onto ribbed tray

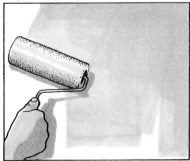

2 Apply in zig-zags, finish in one direction

Applying paint by pad

1 Loading a paint pad
Load the pad evenly by drawing it across the integral roller on the tray without squeezing.

Paint pads for large surfaces have flat rectangular faces covered with a short mohair pile. A plastic-foam backing gives the pad flexibility so that the pile will always be in contact with the wall, even on a rough surface.

The exact size of the pad will be determined by the brand you choose, but one about 200mm (8in) long is best for applying paint evenly and smoothly to walls and ceilings. You will also need a small pad or paintbrush for cutting in at corners and ceilings.

Loading a pad

Load a pad from its own special tray, drawing the pad across the captive roller so that you pick up an even amount of paint (1).

Using a pad

To apply the paint consistently, keep the pad flat on the wall and sweep it gently and evenly in any direction (2). Use criss-cross strokes for emulsion, but finish oil paints with vertical strokes to prevent streaking.

2 Sweep pad gently in any direction

Even the most experienced decorator can't help dripping a little paint, so always paint the ceiling before the walls. Erect a work platform so you can cover as much of the surface as possible without changing position: you will achieve a better finish and will be able to work in safety. Choose your tools wisely and follow a strict working routine for the best effects. Refer to the chart below for professional results.

● Black dot denotes compatibility.
All surfaces must be clean, sound, dry and free from organic growth.

FINISHES FOR INTERIOR WALLS & CEILINGS

	Emulsion	One-coat emulsion	New-plaster emulsion	Solvent-based paint	Acrylic paint	Textured paint	Cement paint
SUITABLE TO COVER							
Plaster	●	●	●	●	●	●	●
Wallpaper	●	●	●	●	●		
Brick	●	●	●	●	●	●	●
Stone	●	●	●	●	●	●	●
Concrete	●	●	●	●	●	●	●
Previously painted surface	●	●	●	●	●	●	
DRYING TIME: HOURS							
Touch dry	1–2	3–4	1–2	2–4	1–2	24	1–2
Recoatable	4		4	16–18	4		24
THINNERS: SOLVENTS							
Water	●	●	●		●	●	●
White spirit				●			
NUMBER OF COATS							
Normal conditions	2	1	2	1–2	1–2	1	2
COVERAGE: APPROXIMATE							
Sq metres per litre	9–15	8	11	15–16	10–14	2–3	
Sq metres per kg							1–6
METHOD OF APPLICATION							
Brush	●	●	●	●	●	●	●
Roller	●	●	●	●	●	●	●
Spray gun	●	●	●	●	●		

Painting the walls

Use a small brush to paint the edges, starting at a top corner of the room. If you are right-handed work from right to left and vice versa. Paint an area of about 600mm (2ft) square at a time. When using emulsion, paint in horizontal bands (**1**), but with gloss paints use vertical strips (**2**) as the junctions are more likely to show unless you blend in the wet edges quickly. Always finish a complete wall before you take a break as otherwise a change of tone will show between separate painted sections.

1 Paint emulsion in horizontal bands

2 Apply oil paints in vertical strips

Painting the ceiling

Start in a corner near the window and carefully paint along the edges with a small paintbrush.

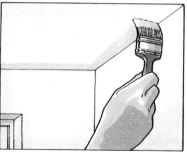
Paint around the edges first

Working from the wet edges, paint in 600mm (2ft) wide bands, working away from the light. Whether you use a brush, pad or a roller, apply each fresh load of paint just clear of the previous application, then blend in the junctions for even coverage.

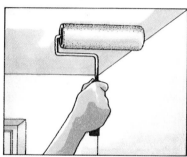
Blend in the wet edges

Electrical fittings

Unscrew a ceiling-rose cover so that you can paint right up to the backplate with a small brush. Loosen the faceplate or mounting box of sockets and switches to paint behind them.

Remember: switch off at the mains before exposing electrical connections.

Unscrew rose cover to keep it clean

FINISHING
WOODWORK

Paint is the usual finish for woodwork in and around the house, offering as it does a protective coating in a choice of colours and surface finishes. However, stains, varnishes and polishes can also be used to give an attractive, durable finish to joinery. They enable you to add colour to woodwork without obliterating the natural beauty of its grain, while transparent finishes are a good alternative where you don't want to alter the natural wood colour. Bear in mind the location of the woodwork and the amount of wear it is likely to get when choosing a finish.

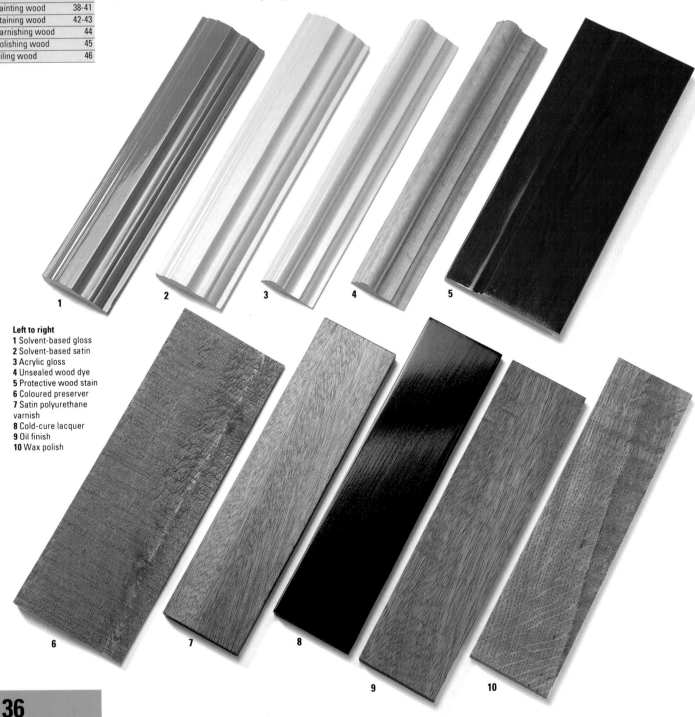

Left to right
1 Solvent-based gloss
2 Solvent-based satin
3 Acrylic gloss
4 Unsealed wood dye
5 Protective wood stain
6 Coloured preserver
7 Satin polyurethane varnish
8 Cold-cure lacquer
9 Oil finish
10 Wax polish

THE CHOICE OF FINISHES FOR WOOD

SEE ALSO
Details for:
Primers 21

The list below gives a comprehensive range of finishes for decorating and protecting woodwork. Each has qualities which render it suitable for a particular purpose, although many can be employed simply for their attractive appearance rather than for any practical considerations. However, this does depend on the location of the timberwork, as some finishes are much more durable than others.

WOOD FINISHES

Solvent-based paints
Traditional solvent-based paints (oil paints) are available as high-gloss and satin finishes with both liquid and thixotropic consistencies. Indoors, they last for years with only the occasional wash down to remove finger marks. One or two undercoats are essential, especially outside where durability is reduced considerably by the action of sun and rain: you should consider redecorating every three to four years.

A one-coat paint, with its creamy consistency and high-pigment content, can protect primed wood or obliterate existing colours without undercoating. Apply it liberally and allow it to flow freely rather than brushing it out like a conventional oil paint.

Low-odour solvent-based finishes have largely eradicated the smell and fumes associated with drying paint.

Acrylic paints
Acrylic paints have several advantages over conventional oil paint. Being water-based, they are non-flammable, practically odourless, and constitute less of a risk to health and the environment. They also dry very quickly, so that a job can often be completed in one day. However, this means you have to work swiftly when decorating outside in direct sunlight to avoid leaving brush marks in the rapidly drying paintwork.

Provided they are applied to adequately prepared wood or keyed paintwork, acrylic paints form a tough yet flexible coating that resists cracking and peeling. However, in common with other water-borne finishes, acrylic paints will not dry satisfactorily if they are applied on a damp or humid day. Even under perfect conditions, don't expect to achieve a high-gloss finish.

Wood dyes
Unlike paint, which after the initial priming coat rests on the surface of timber, a dye penetrates the wood. Its main advantage is to enhance the natural colour of the woodwork or to unify the slight variation in colour found in even the same species.

Water-based or oil-based dyes are available ready for use, and powdered pigments are available for mixing with methylated spirit. None of these dyes will actually protect the timber and you will have to seal them with a clear varnish or polish.

Protective wood stains
The natural colour of wood can be enhanced with protective wood stains. Being moisture-vapour permeable, they allow the wood to breathe while providing a weather-resistant satin finish that resists flaking and peeling.

Protective wood stains are invariably brushed onto the wood. Some manufacturers recommend two to three coats, while others offer a one-coat finish. Some ranges include a clear finish for redecorating previously stained woodwork without darkening the existing colour. Generally, water-based stains tend to dry faster than those thinned with a spirit solvent.

Coloured preservers
Sawn-timber fencing, wall cladding and outbuildings look particularly unattractive when painted, yet they need protection. Use a wood preserver, which penetrates deeply into the timber to prevent rot and insect attack. There are clear preservers, plus a range of natural-wood colours.

Traditional preservers, especially creosote, have a strong, unpleasant smell and are harmful to plants, but most modern low-odour solvent-based and water-based preservers are perfectly safe, even for greenhouses and propagators.

Varnishes
Varnish is a clear protective coating for timber. Most modern varnishes are made with polyurethane resins to provide a waterproof, scratchproof and heat-resistant finish. Most are ready to apply, although some are supplied with a catalyst which must be added before the varnish is used. They come in high-gloss, satin or matt finishes.

An exterior-grade varnish is more weather-resistant. Yacht varnish, which is formulated to withstand even salt water, would be an ideal finish for exterior woodwork in a coastal climate.

Some varnishes are designed to provide a clear finish with a hint of colour. They are available in the normal wood shades and some strong colours. Unlike a wood dye a coloured varnish does not sink into the timber, so there may be loss of colour in areas of heavy wear or abrasion unless you apply additional coats of clear varnish.

Fast-drying acrylic varnishes have an opaque, milky appearance when applied, but are clear and transparent when dry.

Cold-cure lacquer
Cold-cure lacquer is a plastic coating which is mixed with a hardener just before it is used. It is extremely durable (even on floors) and is resistant to heat and alcohol. The standard type dries to a high gloss, which can be burnished to a lacquer-like finish if required. There is also a matt-finish grade, but a smoother matt surface can be obtained by rubbing down the gloss coating with fine steel wool dipped in wax. Cold-cure lacquer is available in clear, black or white.

Oil
Oil is a subtle finish which soaks into the wood, leaving a mellow sheen on the surface. Traditional linseed oil remains sticky for hours, but a modern oil will dry in about an hour and provides a tougher, more durable finish. Oil can be used on softwood as well as open-grained oily hardwoods, such as teak or afrormosia. It is suitable for interior and exterior woodwork.

Wax polishes
Wax can be used to preserve and maintain another finish or as a finish itself. A good wax should be a blend of beeswax and a hard polishing wax such as carnauba. Some contain silicones to make it easier to achieve a high gloss.

Wax polish may be white or tinted various shades of brown to darken the wood. Although it is very attractive, it is not a durable finish and should be used indoors only.

French polish
French polish is a specialized wood finish made by dissolving shellac in alcohol. It is easily scratched and alcohol, even water, will etch the surface, leaving white stains. Consequently, it can be used only on furniture unlikely to receive normal wear and tear.

There are several varieties. Reddish-brown button polish is the best-quality standard polish. It is bleached to make white polish for light-coloured woods and if the natural wax is removed from the shellac, a transparent polish is produced. For mahogany, choose a dark-red garnet polish.

1 Button polish
2 Garnet polish
3 White polish

PAINTING WOODWORK

● **Removing a blemish**
If you find specks of fluff or a brush bristle embedded in fresh paintwork, don't attempt to remove them once a skin has begun to form on the paint. Let it harden, then rub down with wet-and-dry paper. The same applies if you discover runs.

When you are painting wood, take into account the fact that it is a fibrous material which has a definite grain pattern, different rates of absorbency and knots that may possibly ooze resin – all qualities that will have a bearing on the type of paint you will use as well as the techniques and tools you will need to apply it.

Basic application

Always prepare and prime all new woodwork thoroughly before applying the finishing coats.

If you are using conventional oil paint, apply one or two undercoats, depending on the covering power of the paint. As each coat hardens, rub down with fine wet-and-dry paper to remove blemishes and wipe the surface with a cloth dampened with white spirit.

Apply the paint with vertical strokes, then spread it sideways to even out the coverage. Finish with light strokes (laying off) in the direction of the grain. Blend the edges of the next application while the paint is still wet. Don't go back over a painted surface that has started to dry, or you will leave brush marks in the paintwork.

Use a different technique for spreading one-coat or acrylic paints: simply lay on the paint liberally with almost parallel strokes, then lay off lightly. Blend wet edges quickly.

Best-quality paintbrushes are the most efficient tools for painting woodwork. You will need 25 and 50mm (1 and 2in) brushes for general work and a 12mm (½in) paintbrush for painting narrow glazing bars.

Painting a panel
When painting up to the edge of a panel, brush from the centre out: if you flex the bristles against the edge, the paint will run.

● Black dot denotes compatibility. All surfaces must be clean, sound, dry and free from organic growth.

Similarly, mouldings flex the bristles unevenly and too much paint flows: spread it well, taking care at corners of moulded panels.

Making a straight edge
To finish an area with a straight edge, use one of the smaller brushes and place it a few millimetres from the edge. As you flex the bristles they will spread to the required width, laying on an even coat of paint.

THE ORDER OF WORK

Using fast-drying paints you may be able to complete a job in one day, but if you are using conventional solvent-based paints plan your work to make sure the paint will be dry enough to close doors and windows by nightfall.

Inside

Paint windows early, followed by doors and picture rails. Finish with skirting boards so that any specks of dust picked up on the brush will not be transferred to other areas.

Outside

Don't paint in direct sunlight as it dries water-based paints too quickly and creates glare from pale colours.

Never paint on wet or windy days: rain specks will pit the finish and airborne dust will ruin it.

FINISHES FOR WOODWORK

	Solvent-based paint	Acrylic paint	Wood dye	Protective wood stain	Coloured preserver	Varnish	Acrylic varnish	Cold-cure lacquer	Oil	Wax polish	French polish
SUITABLE TO COVER											
Softwoods	●	●	●	●	●	●	●	●	●	●	
Hardwoods	●	●	●	●	●	●	●	●	●	●	●
Oily hardwoods	●	●	●	●		●	●	●	●	●	●
Planed wood	●	●	●	●		●	●	●	●	●	●
Sawn wood					●						
Interior use	●	●	●	●		●	●	●	●	●	●
Exterior use	●	●		●	●	●	●	●			
DRYING TIME: HOURS											
Touch-dry	4	1–2	0.5	0.5–4	1–2	2–4	0.5	1	1		0.5
Recoatable	16	4–6	6	4–16	2–4	14	2	2	6	1	24
THINNERS: SOLVENTS											
Water		●	●	●	●		●				
White spirit	●		●	●	●	●			●	●	
Methylated spirit											●
Special thinner								●			
NUMBER OF COATS											
Interior use	1–2	1–2	2–3	1–2		2–3	3	2–3	3	2	10–15
Exterior use	2–3	1–2		1–2	2	3–4	3–4		3		
COVERAGE											
Sq metres per litre	15–16	10–14	16–30	10–25	4–12	15–16	15–17	16–17	10–15	Variable	Variable
METHOD OF APPLICATION											
Brush	●	●	●	●	●	●	●	●	●	●	●
Paint pad	●	●		●		●	●				
Cloth pad (rubber)			●					●	●	●	●
Spray gun		●				●	●	●	●		

PAINTING
DOORS

Doors have a variety of faces and conflicting grain patterns that need to be painted separately – yet the end result must look even in colour, with no ugly brush marks or heavily painted edges. There are recommended procedures for painting all types of door.

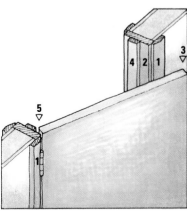

Painting each side with a different colour
Make sure all the surfaces that face you when the door is open are painted the same colour.

Opening side: paint the architrave (1) and door frame up to and including the edge of the door stop (2) one colour. Paint the face of the door and its opening edge (3) the same colour.

Opposite side: paint the architrave and frame up to and over the door stop (4) the second colour. Paint the opposite face of the door and its hinged edge (5) with the second colour.

Preparation and technique

Remove the door handles and wedge the door open so that it cannot be closed accidentally, locking you in the room. Keep the handle in the room with you, just in case.

Aim to paint the door and its frame separately so that there is less chance of touching wet paintwork when passing through a freshly painted doorway. Paint the door first and when it is dry finish the framework.

If you want to use a different colour for each side of the door, paint the hinged edge the colour of the closing face (the one that comes to rest against the frame). Paint the outer edge of the door the same colour as the opening face. This means that there won't be any difference in colour when the door is viewed from either side.

Each side of the frame should match the corresponding face of the door. Paint the frame in the room into which the door swings, including the edge of the stop bead against which the door closes, to match the opening face. Paint the rest of the frame the colour of the closing face.

System for a flush door

To paint a flush door, start at the top and work down in sections, blending each one into the other. Lay on the paint, then finish each section with light vertical brush strokes. Finally, paint the edges. Brush from the edges, never onto them, or the paint will build up and run, forming a ridge.

System for a panelled door

The different parts of a panelled door must be painted in logical order. Finish each part with parallel strokes in the direction of the grain.

Whatever the style of panelled door you are painting, start with the mouldings (1) followed by the panels (2). Paint the centre verticals (muntins) (3) next, then the cross rails (4). Finish the face by painting the outer verticals – the stiles (5). Finally, paint the edge of the door (6).

To achieve a superior finish, paint the muntins, rails and stiles together, picking up the wet edges of the paint before they begin to dry, show brush strokes and pull out bristles. To get the best results you must work quickly.

Glazed doors
To paint a glazed door, begin with the glazing bars, then follow the same sequence as for panelled doors.

Flush door
Apply square sections of paint, working down from the top, and pick up the wet edges for a good blend. Lay off with light vertical brush strokes.

Panelled door: basic painting method
Follow the numbered sequence for painting the various parts of the door, each finished with strokes along the grain to prevent streaking.

Panelled door: advanced painting method
Working rapidly, follow the alternative sequence to produce a finish free from joins between sections.

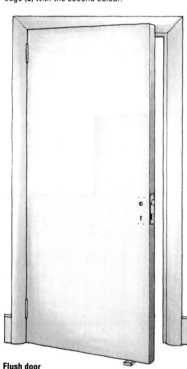

Flush door

Panelled door – basic method

Panelled door – advanced method

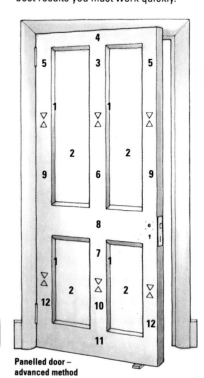

PAINTING WINDOW FRAMES

● **Clean windows first**
Clean the glass in your windows before decorating to avoid picking up particles of dust in the paint.

Cutting-in brush
Paint glazing bars with a cutting-in brush. The bristles are cut at an angle to enable you to work right up to the glass.

● **Painting French windows**
Although French windows are really glazed doors, treat them like large casement windows.

PROTECTING THE GLASS

When painting the edge of glazing bars, overlap the glass by about 2mm (1/16in) to prevent rain or condensation seeping between the glass and woodwork.

If you find it difficult to achieve a satisfactory straight edge, use a proprietary plastic or metal paint shield held against the edge of the frame to protect the glass.

Alternatively, run masking tape around the edges of the window pane, leaving a slight gap so that the paint will seal the join between glass and frame. When the paint is touch-dry, carefully peel off the tape. Don't wait until the paint is completely dry or the film may peel off with the tape.

Once it has set, scrape off any paint that has accidentally dripped onto the glass with a sharp blade. Many DIY stores sell plastic handles to hold blades for this purpose.

Using a paint shield
A plastic or metal paint shield enables you to paint a straight edge up to glass.

KEEPING THE WINDOW OPEN

With the catch and stay removed there's nothing to stop the frame closing. Make a stay with a length of stiff wire, hook the other end and slot it into one of the screw holes in the frame.

Temporary stay
Wind wire around a nail driven in the underside of the frame and use it as a stay.

Like doors, window frames need to be painted in strict order so that the various components will be evenly treated and so that you can close them at night. You also need to take care not to splash window panes with paint or apply a crooked line around the glazing bars – the mark of poor workmanship.

Painting a casement window

A casement window hinges like a door, so if you plan to paint each side a different colour, follow a similar procedure to that described for painting doors and frames.

Remove the stay and catch before you paint the window. So that you can still operate the window during decorating without touching wet paint, drive a nail into the underside of the bottom rail as a makeshift handle.

Painting sequence
First paint the glazing bars (**1**), cutting into the glass on both sides. Carry on with the top and bottom horizontal rails (**2**) followed by the vertical stiles (**3**). Finish the casement by painting the edges (**4**), then paint the frame (**5**).

Painting sequence for casement window ▶

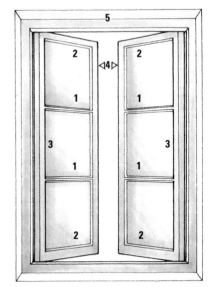

Painting a sash window

Sash windows are the most difficult type to paint, as the two panes slide vertically, overlapping each other.

The following sequence describes the painting of a sash window from the inside. To paint the outside face, use a similar procedure, but start with the lower sash. If you are using different colours for each side, the demarcation lines are fairly obvious: when the window is shut, all the visible surfaces from one side should be the same.

Painting sequence
Raise the bottom sash and pull down the top one. Paint the bottom meeting rail of the top sash (**1**) and the accessible parts of the vertical members (**2**). Reverse the position of the sashes, leaving a gap top and bottom, and complete the painting of the top sash (**3**). Paint the bottom sash (**4**), then the frame (**5**) except for the runners in which the sashes slide.

Leave the paint to dry, then paint the inner runners (**6**) plus a short section of the outer runners (**7**), pulling the cords aside to avoid splashing paint on them as this will make them brittle, shortening their working life. Make sure the window slides before the paint dries.

Raise bottom sash and pull down top

Reverse the position of the sashes

Lower both sashes for access to runners

PAINTING FIXED JOINERY

Staircase

Paint banisters first, making sure that you do not precipitate runs by stroking the brush against the edges or mouldings. Start at the top of the stairs, painting the treads, risers and strings together to keep the edges of the paintwork fresh.

If there is any chance that the paint will not dry before the staircase is used again, paint all the risers, but alternate treads only. The next day, paint the remaining treads.

Skirting boards

The only problem with painting a skirting board is to protect the floor from paint and at the same time avoid picking up dust on the wet paintbrush.

Slide strips of thin card under the skirting as a paint shield (don't use newspaper; it will tear and remain stuck to the skirting).

PAINTING EXTERIOR WEATHERBOARDING

Start at the top of the wall and apply paint to one or two boards at a time. Paint the under-edge first, then the face of the boards; finish parallel with the edge. Make sure you coat exposed end grain well, as it is more absorbent and requires extra protection.

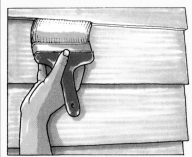

Paint the under-edge of the boards first

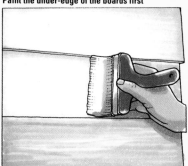

Paint the face of boards next

Graining is a technique for simulating natural wood with paint which was once used extensively on cheap softwood joinery to imitate expensive hardwoods. Doors and panels can look attractive treated in this way. The basic method is simple to describe, but practice on a flat board is essential before you can achieve convincing results. A skilled grainer can simulate actual species of timber, but just try to suggest wood grain rather than attempt to produce a perfect copy.

Equipment and preparation for graining

The simplest graining effects can be achieved by removing dark paint to reveal a paler basecoat below. The traditional way to carry out this effect is to use a special hog's-hair or squirrel-hair brush called a mottler or grainer. To compromise, try trimming a soft-bristled paintbrush or even a dusting brush. You can also buy steel, rubber or leather combs from decorator's suppliers to achieve similar effects.

Applying a base coat (ground)

Prepare the base coat as normal paintwork, finishing with a satin oil paint. It should represent the lightest colour of the timber you want to reproduce and is normally beige or olive green. The base coat will look more convincing if it is slightly dull rather than being too bright.

Choosing the graining colour

Translucent, flat-drying paints are produced especially for graining in a range of appropriate colours. These paints must be thinned with a mixture comprising 2 parts white spirit : 1 part raw linseed oil to make a graining glaze. The quantity of thinner controls the colour of the graining, so add it to the paint sparingly until you achieve the required result. Try the method on a practice panel first.

Producing the effect

Paint an even coat of glaze onto the ground with a 50mm (2in) paintbrush. After only two or three minutes, lightly drag the tip of the mottler or comb along the line of the rail or panel, leaving faints streaks in the glaze.

When two rails meet at right angles, mask the joint with a piece of card to prevent the simulated grain being disturbed on one rail while you paint a rail next to it.

The grain does not have to be exactly parallel with the rail. You can vary the pattern by allowing the comb or mottler to streak out the glaze at a slight angle and over the edge of some of the rails.

Leave the graining to dry overnight, then apply one or two coats of clear varnish to protect and seal the effects.

SEE ALSO

Details for:	
Preparing wood	27
Painting wood	38
Varnishing wood	44

Steel graining comb

Rubber or leather comb

Bristle grainer

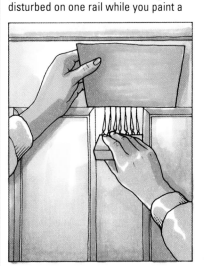

Masking meeting rails
Hold a piece of card over the joint between two meeting rails – for example, where muntins meet cross rails on a panelled door – to avoid spoiling the graining on one while treating the other.

Applying graining patterns
To produce graining patterns that are convincing, run the streaks more or less parallel to the timber, simulating natural wood grain by occasionally running the pattern off at an angle.

41

STAINING
WOODWORK
WITH WOOD DYE

Testing the dye
Make a test strip (far right) to assess the depth of colour of various dyes before embarking on the final job. Apply a band of varnish along the bottom half of the strip to see how the colours are affected.

Paint pad

Paintbrush

Rubber

Unless the wood is perfectly clean and free from grease, wood dye will be rejected, producing an uneven, patchy appearance. Strip any previous finish and sand the wood with progressively finer abrasive papers, always in the direction of the grain. Scratches made across the grain will tend to be emphasized by the dye.

Making a test strip

The final colour is affected by the nature of the timber, the number of coats and the overlying clear finish. You can also mix compatible dyes to alter the colour or dilute them with the appropriate thinner.

Make a test strip so that you will have an accurate guide from which you can choose the depth of colour to suit your purpose. Use a piece of timber from the same batch you are staining, or one that resembles it closely.

Paint the strip with one coat of dye. Allow the dye to be absorbed, then apply a second coat, leaving a strip of the first application showing. It is rarely necessary to apply more than two coats of dye, but for the experiment add a third coat and even a fourth coat, always leaving a strip of the previous application for comparison.

When the dye has dried completely, paint a band of clear varnish along the strip. Some polyurethane varnishes react unfavourably with oil-based dyes, so it is advisable to use products made by the same manufacturer.

USING A RUBBER

Wear gloves to protect your skin and pour some wood dye into a shallow dish. Saturate the rubber with dye, then squeeze some out so that it is not dripping but is still wet enough to apply a liberal coat of dye to the surface.

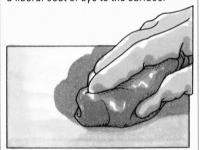

Apply wood dye by rubber

If you wet a piece of timber, water is absorbed by the wood, raising a mass of tiny fibres across the surface. A water-based dye will produce the same result and the final finish will be ruined. Solve the problem by sanding the wood until it is perfectly smooth, then dampen the whole surface with a wet rag. Leave it to dry out, then sand the raised grain with very fine abrasive paper before you begin to apply the dye. If you are

using an oil-based dye, this preliminary process is unnecessary.

If you want to fill the grain, first apply a seal coat of clear finish over the dye. Choose a grain filler that matches the dye closely, adjusting the colour by adding a little dye to it, but make sure that the dye and filler are compatible. An oil-based dye will not mix with a water-based filler and vice versa, so check before you buy either.

How to apply wood dye

Use a 100mm (4in) paintbrush to apply dyes over a wide, flat surface. Do not brush out a dye like paint, but apply it liberally and evenly, always in the direction of the grain.

It is essential to blend wet edges of wood dye, so work fairly quickly and don't take a break until you have completed the job. If you have brushed a water-based dye onto the wood it is sometimes advantageous to wipe over the wet surface with a soft cloth and remove excess dye.

Using a paint pad is one of the best ways of achieving an even coverage of wood dye over a flat surface. However, you may find that you will still need to employ a paintbrush in order to get the dye right into awkward corners and to tackle mouldings.

Because dyes are so fluid, it's often easier to apply them with a wad of soft, lint-free rag called a rubber. You will be able to control runs on a vertical panel and it's the best way to stain turned wood and rails.

Staining a flat panel

Whenever possible, set up a panel horizontally for staining, either on trestles or raised on softwood blocks. Shake the container before use and pour the dye into a flat dish so that you can load your applicator properly.

Apply the dye, working swiftly and evenly along the grain. Stain the edges at the same time as the top surface. The first application may have a slightly patchy appearance as it dries because some parts of the wood will absorb more dye than others. The second coat normally evens out the colour without difficulty. If powdery deposits are left on the surface of the dry wood dye, wipe them off with a coarse, dry cloth before applying the second coat in the same way as the first.

Leave the dye to dry overnight, then proceed with the clear finish of your choice to seal the colourant.

Staining floors

Because a wooden floor is such a large area it is more difficult to blend the wet edges of the dye. Work along two or three boards at a time, using a paintbrush, so that you can finish at the edge of a board each time.

Woodblock floors are even trickier, so it pays to work with an assistant to cover the area quickly, blending and overlapping sections with a soft cloth.

Staining a door

Stain a new or stripped door before it is hung so that it can be layered horizontally. A flush door is stained just like any other panel, but use a rubber to carefully colour the edges so that wood dye does not run underneath to spoil the other side.

When staining a panelled door, it is essential to follow a sequence which will allow you to pick up the wet edges before they dry. Use a combination of brush and rubber to apply the dye.

Follow the numbered sequence below and note that, unlike painting a panelled door, the mouldings are stained last in order to prevent any overlapping showing on the finished door. Stain the mouldings carefully with a narrow brush and blend in the colour with a rubber.

Method for staining a panelled door
Follow this practical sequence, using a combination of paintbrush or paint pad and rubber to apply the dye evenly to the various sections. Start with the inset panels first (**1**), then continue with half of the vertical muntin (**2**), the bottom cross rail (**3**) and half the stiles (**4**). Pick up the wet edges with the other half of the muntin (**5**) and the stiles (**6**). Stain the central cross rail (**7**), then repeat the procedure for the second half of the door (**8–12**), finishing with the mouldings (**13**) using a narrow brush and rubber.

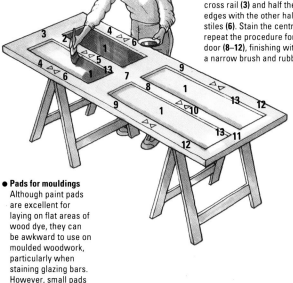

● **Pads for mouldings**
Although paint pads are excellent for laying on flat areas of wood dye, they can be awkward to use on moulded woodwork, particularly when staining glazing bars. However, small pads are made specifically for this purpose.

USING WOOD STAINS OUTSIDE

Standard wood dyes are not suitable for exterior use. They have no protective properties of their own and they have a tendency to fade in direct sunlight. For planed joinery and weatherboarding, use a protective wood stain that is moisture-vapour permeable. For sawn timber use a coloured wood preserver. Both materials are much thinner than paint, so take care to avoid splashing.

Protective wood stain
Make sure all the surface is clean, dry and sanded. All previous paint or varnish must be stripped. For extra protection, treat the timber with a clear wood preserver before staining.

Apply the required number of coats with a paintbrush, making sure that the coverage is even.

Stain wall cladding one board at a time (treating the under-edge first).

Wood preserver
Before you apply a coloured wood preserver, remove surface dirt with a stiff-bristled brush. Paint or varnish must be stripped completely, but previously preserved or creosoted timber can be treated, provided it has weathered.

For additional protection against insect and fungal attack, treat the timber first with a clear wood preserver, either by immersion or by applying full brush coats.

Paint a full coat of coloured preserver onto the wood and, if necessary, follow up with a second coat as soon as the first has soaked in. Brush out sufficiently to achieve an even colour and join all edges swiftly before they have time to dry.

Replacing putty
Stains will not colour old linseed-oil putty so replace it with a coloured plasticized putty, or stain the frame and seal the rebate with mastic (**1**).

Set lengths of stained wooden beading into the mastic and secure them with panel pins (**2**). You will find it easiest to fix the beading if you tap in the pins beforehand, so they just protrude through the other side. Remove excess mastic squeezed from beneath the beading with a putty knife (**3**).

1 Apply mastic

2 Fix beading

3 Trim mastic

43

VARNISHING
WOODWORK

Varnish serves two main purposes: to protect the wood from knocks, stains and other marks, and to give it a sheen that accentuates the beautiful grain pattern. In some cases, it can even be used to change the colour of the wood to that of another species – or to give it a fresh, new look with a choice of bright primary colours.

The effect of varnish
The examples below demonstrate how different varnishes affect the same species of wood. From top to bottom: untreated softwood; matt clear varnish; gloss clear varnish; wood-colour varnish; satin tinted varnish; pure-colour varnish.

How to apply varnish

Use paintbrushes to apply varnish in the same way as paint. You will need a range of sizes for general work: 12, 25 and 50mm (½, 1 and 2in) are useful widths. For varnishing floors, use a 100mm (4in) brush for quick coverage. Whatever size of brush you use, always make sure that it is spotlessly clean; any remaining traces of paint on it may spoil the finish.

Load a brush with varnish by dipping the first third of the bristles into the liquid, then touch off the excess on the side of the container. Don't scrape the brush across the rim of the container as it causes bubbles in the varnish, which can spoil the finish if transferred to the woodwork.

You can employ a soft cloth pad, or rubber, to rub a sealer coat of varnish into the grain. While it's not essential to use a rubber it is a convenient method, especially if you are coating shaped or turned pieces of wood.

Applying the varnish

Thin the first sealer coat of varnish by 10 per cent and rub it well into the wood with a cloth pad in the direction of the grain. Brush on the sealer coat where the rubber is difficult to use.

Apply the second coat of varnish within the stipulated time. If more than 24 hours have elapsed, lightly key the surface of solvent-based gloss varnish with fine abrasive paper. Wipe it over with a cloth dampened with white spirit in order to remove dust and grease, then brush on a full coat of varnish in the same manner as for paint.

Apply a third coat if the surface is likely to take hard wear.

Using coloured varnish

A wood stain can only be used on bare timber, but you can use a coloured varnish to darken or alter the colour of woodwork that has been varnished previously without having to strip the finish. Clean the surface with wire wool and white spirit mixed with a little linseed oil. Dry the surface with a clean cloth, then apply the varnish.

Apply tinted varnish in the same way as the clear type. It might be worth making a test strip to see how many coats you will need to achieve the depth of colour you want.

Varnishing floors

Varnishing a floor is no different from finishing any other woodwork, but if you are using a solvent-based finish the greater area can produce an unpleasant concentration of fumes in a confined space. Open all windows to provide maximum ventilation and wear a respirator.

Start in the corner furthest from the door and work back towards it. Brush the varnish out well to make sure it does not collect in pools.

DEALING WITH DUST PARTICLES

Minor imperfections and particles of dust stuck to the varnished surface can be rubbed down with fine abrasive paper between coats. If your top coat is to be a high-gloss finish, take even more care to ensure that your brush is perfectly clean.

If you are not satisfied with your final finish, wait until it is dry, then dip very fine wire wool in wax polish and rub the varnish with parallel strokes in the direction of the grain. Buff the surface with a soft duster. This treatment removes a high gloss, but it leaves a pleasant sheen on the surface with no obvious imperfections.

Produce a soft sheen with wire wool and wax

The art of French polishing has always been considered the province of the expert, to be left well alone by amateurs. It is true that an expert will make a better job of the polishing and work much faster than an amateur, but there's no reason why anyone cannot produce a satisfactory finish with a little practice.

Woodwork must be prepared immaculately before polishing as every blemish will be mirrored in the finish, so spoiling the effect. The grain should be filled, either with a proprietary filler or with layers of polish, which are rubbed down and recoated until the pores of the wood are eventually filled flush.

Always work in a warm, dust-free room: a low temperature will make the polish go cloudy (bloom) and dust will mar the finish.

Make sure you work in a good light so that you can glance across the surface in order to gauge the quality of the finish you are applying.

BRUSHING FRENCH POLISH

If you haven't the time to practise applying shellac with a rubber, use a special French polish that can be brushed onto the surface. It contains an agent that retards the drying process so that brush marks can flow out before the polish begins to set.

The technique for applying this brushing polish is easy to master. Use a soft paintbrush to apply an even coat, then, after 15 to 20 minutes, rub down lightly with silicon-carbide paper. Paint on two more coats, rubbing down between applications. When the shellac has set, dip a ball of 0000 grade wire wool in soft wax polish and rub it gently up and down the panel, using overlapping parallel strokes.

Leave the wax to harden for five minutes, then burnish vigorously with a soft duster.

Apply an even coat with a paintbrush

Traditional French polishing

With the rubber open in the palm of your hand, pour shellac onto the cotton wool until it is fully charged, but not absolutely saturated. Fold the fabric over the cotton wool and press the rubber against a scrap board to squeeze out the polish, distributing it evenly across the sole or base of the pad. Dip your fingertip in linseed oil and spread it across the sole to act as a lubricant.

Applying the polish
To apply French polish to a flat panel, first make overlapping circular strokes with the rubber, gradually covering the whole surface with shellac. Go over the same surface again, this time using figure-of-eight strokes – varying the strokes ensures an even coverage. Finish with straight, overlapping strokes parallel with the grain.

Very little pressure is required with a freshly charged rubber, but you need to increase the pressure gradually as the work proceeds. Recharge the cotton wool with polish as necessary, adding another spot of linseed oil to the sole when the rubber starts to drag.

Keep the rubber on the move, sweeping it on and off the wood at the beginning and end of each complete coverage. If you stop with the rubber in contact with the work the pad will stick to the polish, leaving a scar. In this event, let the shellac harden thoroughly and rub it down with very fine self-lubricating silicon-carbide paper.

Assuming the first complete application is free from blemishes, leave it to dry for 30 minutes, then repeat the process. Build up four to five coats in the same way and leave the polish to harden overnight.

Next day, sand out any dust, runs or rubber marks with silicon-carbide paper before applying four or five coats of polish. In all, 10 to 20 coats will be needed to build a protective coating with the required depth of colour.

Spiriting-off
The linseed-oil lubricant leaves streaks in the polish that have to be removed with a rubber that is practically empty of shellac, but with a few drops of methylated spirit on the sole. Apply the rubber to the polished surface, using straight parallel strokes only, gliding on and off the panel at the beginning and end of each stroke. Recharge the rubber with more methylated spirit as soon as it begins to drag. Leave the work for a minute or two, and repeat the process if the streaks reappear. Spiriting off not only removes streaking but eventually burnishes the French polish to a glass-like finish.

Half an hour later, buff the surface with a soft duster, then leave it to harden for at least a week.

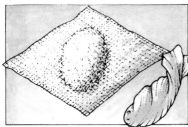

Making a rubber
Traditionally, French polish is applied with a soft pad known as a rubber. To make one, take a handful of cotton wool and squeeze it roughly egg-shaped, then place it in the centre of a 300mm (1ft) square of white linen. Fold the fabric over the cotton wool, gathering the loose material in the palm of your hand. Smooth out any wrinkles across the sole of the pad.

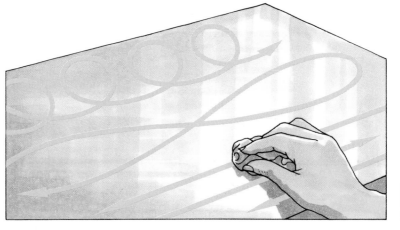

Using the rubber
Apply the polish with a combination of circular and figure-of-eight strokes so that every part of the surface is covered. When you finish each coat, run the rubber in long straight strokes, parallel to the wood grain. Keep your rubber pliable by storing it in a screw-top jar overnight.

COLD-CURE
LACQUER

Due to its chemical composition, careful preparation is essential or cold-cure lacquer will take days to cure instead of only two hours. It must be applied to a clean, grease-free surface, which has been sanded smooth. Strip the old finish, but do not use a caustic stripper, as this will react against the coating.

Clean old wax polish from the wood. You must remove every trace, even from the pores of the timber. Wash it with white spirit, using a ball of fine wire wool in the direction of the grain. When the wood is dry, scrub it with water and detergent, then rinse the surface with clean water with a little white vinegar added.

If you use wood dye, make sure it is made by the manufacturer of the lacquer, otherwise it might change colour. Use the same manufacturer's stopping to fill cracks and holes and never use plaster or plastic fillers.

Mixing cold-cure lacquer

In most cases using a paintbrush is the best method of applying plastic coating, although you can use a plastic-foam roller instead, especially for large areas of woodwork.

When you are ready to apply the lacquer, mix the coating and hardener in a glass or polyethylene container. Use the proportions recommended by the manufacturer. Mix just enough for your needs, as it will set in two to three days in an open dish. Don't be tempted to try to economize by pouring the mixed lacquer back into its original container as the hardener will completely ruin any remaining substance therein.

Applying the lacquer

Cold-cure lacquer must be applied in a warm atmosphere. Use a well-loaded applicator and spread the lacquer onto the wood. There is no need to brush out the liquid as it will flow unaided and even a thick coat will cure thoroughly and smoothly. The lacquer dries quickly and will begin to show brush marks if it is disturbed after 10 to 15 minutes, so you should work swiftly in order to pick up the wet edges.

After two hours, apply the second coat. If necessary, rub down the hardened lacquer with fine abrasive paper to remove blemishes, then add a third coat. You will achieve better adhesion between the layers if you can apply all the coats in one day, as long as each has time to dry.

Burnishing lacquer

If you want a mirror finish, wait for 24 hours, then use a proprietary burnishing cream. Rub down the lacquer with very fine abrasive paper or wire wool, then rub the cream onto the surface with a soft cloth. Burnish it vigorously with a clean soft duster to achieve the required depth of sheen.

Matting lacquer

To produce a subtle satin coat, rub the hardened lacquer along the grain with fine wire wool dipped in wax polish. The grade of the wire wool will affect the degree of matting. Use fine 000 grade for a satin finish and a coarse 0 grade for a fully-matted surface. Polish with a clean, soft duster.

SAFETY WHEN USING LACQUER

Although cold-cure lacquer is safe to use, take care when applying it to a large surface such as a floor as there will be a concentration of fumes.

Open all windows and doors if possible for ventilation – but remember the necessity for a warm atmosphere, too – and take the extra precaution of wearing a respirator to prevent you breathing in the fumes. The hardener is acidic, so wash thoroughly with water if you spill any on your skin.

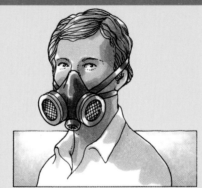

● **Spontaneous combustion**
It is essential to dispose of oily rags immediately you have finished with them as they have been known to burst into flames.

OILING AND
WAXING WOODWORK

Applying the oil

Clean and prepare the wood for oiling. Remove previous finishes carefully so that oil can penetrate the grain.

The most efficient way to apply a finishing oil is to rub it into the wood with a soft, lint-free rag in the form of a rubber. Don't store oily rags: keep them in a sealed tin while the job is in progress, then unfold them and leave them outside to dry before throwing them away.

A brush is a convenient way to spread oil liberally over large surfaces and into carvings or deep mouldings.

Rub or brush a generous coating of oil into the wood grain. Leave it to soak in for a few minutes, then rub off excess oil with a clean cloth. After about six hours, coat the wood with oil once more. The next day, apply a third and final coat; raise a faint sheen by burnishing with a soft duster.

Wax-polishing timber

If you want to wax-polish new timber, seal the wood first with one coat of clear varnish (or French polish on fine furniture). This will stop the wax being absorbed too deeply into the wood and provides a slightly more durable finish. Before waxing an old clear finish, clean it first to remove deposits of dirt and possibly an old wax dressing.

To remove dirty wax, mix up white spirit with 25 per cent linseed oil. Use the liquid to clean the surface vigorously with a coarse cloth. If there is no obvious improvement, try dipping very fine wire wool into the cleaner and rub in the direction of the grain. Don't press too hard as you want only to remove wax and dirt without damaging the finish below. Wash the cleaned surface with a cloth dipped in white spirit and leave to dry before refinishing.

Wax polish can be applied with a soft cloth, but when using liquid wax it's best to employ a paintbrush to seal the wood with it first. Then pour the liquid wax onto a cloth pad and rub it in with a circular motion, followed by strokes parallel with the grain. Make this first coat a generous one.

Buff up the wax after one hour, then apply a second, thinner coat in the direction of the grain only. Burnish this coat lightly and leave for several hours to harden. Bring to a high gloss by burnishing vigorously with a soft duster.

Ferrous metals that are rusty will shed practically any paint film rapidly, so the most important aspect of finishing metalwork is thorough preparation and priming to prevent this corrosion from returning; after that, applying the finish is virtually the same as painting woodwork.

When you are choosing a finish for metalwork in and around the house, make sure it fulfils your requirements (see chart below and table overleaf for suitable types). Many of the finishes listed are easy to apply to metal, but the ability of some to withstand heavy wear is likely to be poor.

Methods of application

Most of the finishes suggested for use on metalwork can be applied with a paintbrush. The exception is black lead. In general, use the standard techniques for painting woodwork, except that bitumen-based paints should be laid on only and not brushed out as are conventional coatings.

Remove metal door and window fittings for painting, suspending them on wire hooks to dry. Make sure that sharp edges are coated properly, as the finish can wear thin relatively quickly.

Some paints can be sprayed, but there are few situations where this is advantageous, except perhaps in the case of intricately moulded ironwork such as garden furniture, which you can paint outside. Indoors, ventilation is a necessity.

A roller is suitable for large flat surfaces. Pipework requires its own special V-section roller, which is designed to coat curved surfaces.

● Black dot denotes compatibility.
All surfaces must be clean, sound, dry and free from organic growth.

FINISHES FOR METALWORK

	Solvent-based paint	Hammered-finish paint	Metallic paint	Bitumen-based paint	Security paint	Radiator enamel	Black lead	Lacquer	Bath paint	Non-slip paint
DRYING TIME: HOURS										
Touch-dry	4	0.5	4	1–2		2–6		0.25	6–10	4–6
Recoatable	14	1–3	8	6–24		7–14			16–24	12
THINNERS: SOLVENTS										
Water				●						
White spirit	●		●	●	●		●		●	●
Special		●				●				
Cellulose thinners								●		
NUMBER OF COATS										
Normal conditions	1–2	1	1–2	1–3	1	1–2	Variable	1	2	2
COVERAGE										
Sq metres per litre	12–16	3–5	10–14	6–15	2.5	13	Variable	18	13–14	3–5
METHOD OF APPLICATION										
Brush	●	●	●	●	●	●	●	●	●	●
Paint pad	●	●		●						
Spray gun	●	●		●				●		
Cloth pad (rubber)							●			

PAINTING RADIATORS AND PIPES

Leave radiators and hot-water pipes to cool before you paint them. The only problem with decorating a radiator is how to paint the back: the best solution is to remove it completely or, if possible, swing it away from the wall. After you have painted the back, reposition the radiator and paint the front.

If this is inconvenient, use a special radiator brush with a long metal handle (see right). Use the same tool to paint in between the leaves of a double radiator. It is difficult to achieve a perfect finish even with the brush, so aim at covering areas you are likely to see when the radiator is fixed in position rather than a complete application.

Don't paint over radiator valves or fittings or you will not be able to operate them afterwards.

Paint pipework lengthwise rather than across, or runs are likely to form. The first coat on metal piping will be streaky, so be prepared to apply two or three coats. Unless you are using radiator enamel, allow the paint to harden thoroughly before turning on the heat, or it may blister.

Using a radiator brush
A long, slim-handled radiator brush enables you to paint the back of the radiator without having to remove it from the wall. You can also use this brush to paint between the leaves of a double radiator.

METALWORK

1 Protect wall
Use card behind a downpipe when painting behind it.

2 Apply lacquer
Use a large, soft artist's paintbrush.

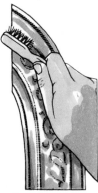

3 Apply black lead
Scrub cream into intricate surfaces using an old toothbrush.

Gutters and downpipes

It is best to coat the inside of gutters with a bitumen-based paint for thorough protection against moisture, but you can finish the outer surfaces with oil paint or security paint.

To protect the wall behind a downpipe, slip a scrap of card between while painting the back of the pipe (1).

Metal casement windows

Paint metal casement windows using the sequence described for wooden casements, which allows you to close the frame at night without spoiling a freshly-painted surface.

Lacquering metalwork

Polish the metal to a high gloss, then use a nail brush to scrub it with warm water containing some liquid detergent. Rinse the metal in clean water, then dry it thoroughly with an absorbent cloth.

Paint on acrylic lacquer with a large, soft, artist's brush (2), working swiftly from the top. Let the lacquer flow naturally, and work all round the object to keep the wet edge moving.

If you do leave a brush stroke in partially-set lacquer, finish the job, then warm the metal (by standing it on a radiator if possible). As soon as the blemish disappears, remove the object from the heat and allow it to cool gradually in a dust-free atmosphere.

Blacking cast iron

Black lead produces an attractive finish for cast iron. It is not a permanent or durable finish and will have to be renewed periodically. It may transfer if rubbed hard.

Black lead is supplied in a toothpaste-like tube. Squeeze some onto a soft cloth and spread it onto the metal. Use an old toothbrush (3) to scrub it into decorative ironwork for best coverage.

When you have covered the surface, buff it to a satin sheen with a clean, dry cloth. Build up several applications of black lead to give a patina and a moisture-resistant finish.

SUITABLE FINISHES FOR METALWORK

Solvent-based paints

Conventional solvent-based paints are perfectly usable on metal. Once it has been primed, interior metalwork will need at least one undercoat plus a top coat. Add an extra undercoat to protect exterior metalwork.

Hammered-finish paint

A combination of heat-hardened glass flakes, aluminium particles and resins, hammered-finish paint is applied as one coat only. There's no need for primer or undercoat, even when painting previously rusted metal. A smooth-finish paint with the same properties is also available.

Metallic paints

For a metallic-like finish, choose a paint containing aluminium, copper, gold or bronze powders. These paints are water-resistant and are able to withstand very high temperatures – up to about 100°C (212°F).

Bitumen-based paints

Bitumen-based paints give economical protection for exterior storage tanks and piping. Standard bituminous paint is black, but there is also a limited range of colours, plus 'modified' bituminous paint, which contains aluminium.

Security paints

Non-setting security paint, primarily for rainwater and waste downpipes, remains slippery to prevent intruders from scaling the wall via the pipe. Restrict it to pipework over about 2m (6ft) above the ground.

Radiator enamels

Radiator enamel is a heat-stoving acrylic paint that is applied in two thin coats. A choice of satin and gloss finishes is available.

Radiator enamel can be used over emulsion or oil paints as long as these have not been recently applied (don't rub them down first). Apply a compatible metal primer over new paint or factory priming to stop solvents in the enamel reacting with the previous coating (this does not apply to water-based radiator enamel). A special thinner is normally required for brush cleaning.

Finish the radiator in position, then turn the heating on (set to maximum) for a minimum of two hours to bake the enamel onto the metal. Apply a second coat six to eight hours later.

You can also use radiator enamel to repaint boiler cabinets, refrigerators, cookers and washing machines.

Black lead

A cream used for cast ironwork, black lead is a mixture of graphite and waxes. It is reasonably moisture-resistant, but is not suitable for exterior use.

Lacquer

Virtually any clear lacquer can be used on polished metalwork without spoiling its appearance, but many polyurethanes yellow with age. A clear acrylic metal lacquer will protect chrome-plating, brass and copper – even outside.

Non-slip paints

Designed to provide good foot-holding on a wide range of surfaces, including metal, non-slip paint is ideal for painting metal staircase treads and exterior fire escapes. The surface must be primed before application.

APPLYING TEXTURED COATING

You can apply the coating with either a roller or broad wall brush: finer textures are possible using the latter. Buy a special roller if recommended by the coating manufacturer.

With a well-loaded roller, apply a generous coat in a 600mm (2ft) wide band across the ceiling or down a wall. Do not press too hard and vary the angle of the stroke.

If you decide to brush on the coating, do not spread it out like paint. Lay it on with one stroke and spread it back again with one or two strokes only.

Texture the first band, then apply a second band and blend them together before texturing the latter. Continue in this way until the wall or ceiling is complete. Keep the room ventilated until the coating has hardened.

Painting around fittings
Use a small paintbrush to fill in around electrical fittings and along edges, trying to copy the texture used on the surrounding wall or ceiling. Some people prefer to form a distinct margin around fittings by drawing a small paintbrush along the perimeter to give a smooth finish.

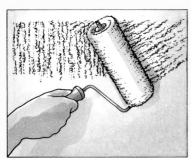

Creating a texture
You can experiment with a variety of tools to make any number of textures. Try a coarse expanded-foam roller or one made with a special surface to produce diagonal or diamond patterns; alternatively, apply a swirling, ripple or stipple finish with improvised equipment, as shown on the right.

Textured coatings can be obtained as a dry powder for mixing with warm water or in a ready-mixed form for direct application from the tub. They are available in a range of standard colours, but if none of them suit your decorative scheme you can use ordinary emulsion as a finish. Textured coatings are suitable for both exterior and interior walls.

Using rollers, scrapers or improvised tools, you can produce a variety of textures. It pays to restrict distinctly raised textures with sharp edges to areas where you are unlikely to rub against the wall. Create finer textures for children's rooms, small bathrooms and narrow hallways.

Preparing for textured coatings

New surfaces will need virtually no preparation, but joints between plasterboard must be reinforced with tape. Strip any wallcoverings and key gloss paint with glasspaper. Old walls and ceilings must be clean, dry, sound and free from organic growth. Treat friable surfaces with stabilizing solution.

Although large cracks and holes must be filled, a textured coating will conceal minor defects in walls and ceilings by filling small cracks and bridging shallow bumps and hollows.

Masking joinery and fittings
Use 50mm (2in) wide masking tape to cover doorframes and window frames, electrical fittings, plumbing pipework, picture rails and skirting boards. Lay dust sheets over the floor.

1 Diamond pattern

2 Stipple effect

3 Swirl design

4 Combed arcs

5 Tree-bark simulation

6 Stucco finish

1 Geometric patterns
Use a roller with diamond or diagonal grooves: load the roller and draw lightly across the textured surface.

2 Stippled finish
Pat the coating with a damp sponge to create a pitted profile. Rinse out frequently. Alter your wrist angle and overlap sections.

3 Random swirls
Twist a damp sponge on the textured surface, then pull away to make a swirling design. Overlap swirls for a layered effect.

4 Combed arcs
A toothed spatula sold with the finish is employed to create combed patterns: arcs, criss-cross patterns or wavy scrolls.

5 Imitation tree bark
Produce a bark texture by applying parallel strokes with a roller, then lightly drawing the straight edge of a spatula over it.

6 Stucco finish
Apply parallel roller strokes, then run the rounded corner of a spatula over it in short straight strokes.

WALLCOVERINGS

Top right
1 Expanded polystyrene
2 Lining paper
3 Woodchip

Bottom left
4 Hand-printed
5 Machine-printed

Bottom right
6 Lincrusta
7 Embossed-paper wallcovering
8 Blown vinyl

Although wallcoverings are often called 'wallpaper', only a proportion of the wide range available is made solely from wood pulp. There is a huge range of paper-backed fabrics from exotic silks to coarse hessians; other types include natural textures such as cork or woven grass on a paper backing. Plastics have widened the choice of wallcoverings still further: there are paper-backed or cotton-backed vinyls, and plain or patterned foamed plastics. Before wallpaper became popular fabric wall hangings were used to decorate interiors and this is still done today, using unbacked fabrics glued or stretched across walls.

Ensuring a suitable surface

Although many wallcoverings will cover minor blemishes, walls and ceilings should be clean, sound and smooth. Eradicate damp and organic growth before hanging any wallcovering. Consider whether you should size the walls to reduce paste absorption.

COVERINGS THAT CAMOUFLAGE

Although a poor surface should be repaired, some coverings hide minor blemishes as well as providing a foundation for other finishes.

Expanded-polystyrene sheet
Thin polystyrene sheet is used for lining a wall before papering. It reduces condensation and also bridges hairline cracks and small holes. Polystyrene dents easily, so don't use where it will take a lot of punishment. There is a patterned version for ceilings.

Lining paper
A cheap, buff-coloured wallpaper for lining uneven or impervious walls prior to hanging a heavy or expensive wallcovering. It also provides an even surface for emulsion paint.

Woodchip paper
Woodchip or ingrain paper is a relief covering made by sandwiching particles of wood between two layers of paper. It is inexpensive, easy to hang (but a problem to cut), and must be painted.

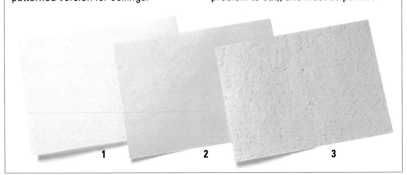

1   2   3

Printed wallpapers
One advantage of ordinary wallpaper is the superb range of printed colours and patterns, which is much wider than for any other covering. Most papers – the cheapest – are machine-printed.

The more costly hand-printed papers are prone to tearing when wet and the inks have a tendency to run if you smear paste on the surface. They are not really suitable for walls exposed to wear or condensation. Pattern matching can be awkward, because hand-printing isn't as accurate as machine printing.

Relief papers
Relief papers with deeply embossed patterns hide minor imperfections. Reliefs are invariably painted with emulsion, satin-finish oil paints or water-based acrylics.

The original embossed wallcovering, Lincrusta, consists of a solid film of linseed oil and fillers fused onto a backing paper before the pattern is applied with an engraved steel roller. It is still available, though many people prefer embossed-paper wallcoverings or the superior-quality versions made from cotton fibres. Lightweight vinyl reliefs are also popular. During manufacture, they are heated in an oven which 'blows' or expands the vinyl, creating deeply embossed patterns.

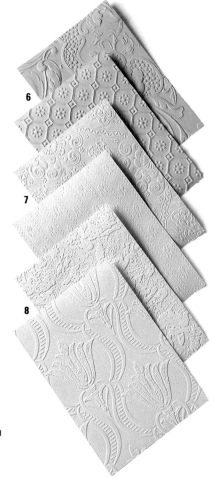

WALLCOVERINGS

Washable papers

These are printed papers with a thin impervious glaze of PVA to make a spongeable surface. Washables are suitable for bathrooms and kitchens. The surface must not be scrubbed or the plastic coating will be worn away.

Vinyl wallcoverings

A base paper, or sometimes a cotton backing, is coated with a layer of vinyl upon which the design is printed. Heat is used to fuse the colours and vinyl. The result is a durable, washable wallcovering ideally suited to bathrooms and kitchens. Many vinyls are sold ready-pasted for easy application.

Foamed-polyethylene covering

This is a lightweight wallcovering made solely of foamed plastic with no backing paper. It is printed with a wide range of patterns, colours and designs. You paste the wall instead of the covering. It is best used on walls that are not exposed to wear.

Flock wallcoverings

Flock papers have the major pattern elements picked out with a fine pile produced by gluing synthetic or natural fibres (such as silk or wool) to the backing paper: the pattern stands out in relief, with a velvet-like texture.

Standard flock papers are difficult to hang, as contact with paste will ruin the pile. Vinyl flocks are less delicate, can be hung anywhere, and may even come ready-pasted.

You can sponge flock paper to remove stains, but brush to remove dust from the pile. Vinyl flocks can be washed without risk of damage.

Grass cloth

Natural grasses are woven into a mat and glued to a paper backing. While these wallcoverings are very attractive, they are fragile and difficult to hang.

Cork-faced paper

This is surfaced with thin sheets of coloured or natural cork. It is not as easily spoiled as other special papers.

Paper-backed fabrics

Finely woven cotton, linen or silk on a paper backing must be applied to a flat surface. They are expensive, not easy to hang, and you must avoid smearing the fabric with adhesive. Most fabrics are delicate, but some are plastic-coated to make them scuff-resistant.

Unbacked fabrics

Upholstery-width fabric – typically hessian – can be wrapped around panels which are then glued or pinned to the wall.

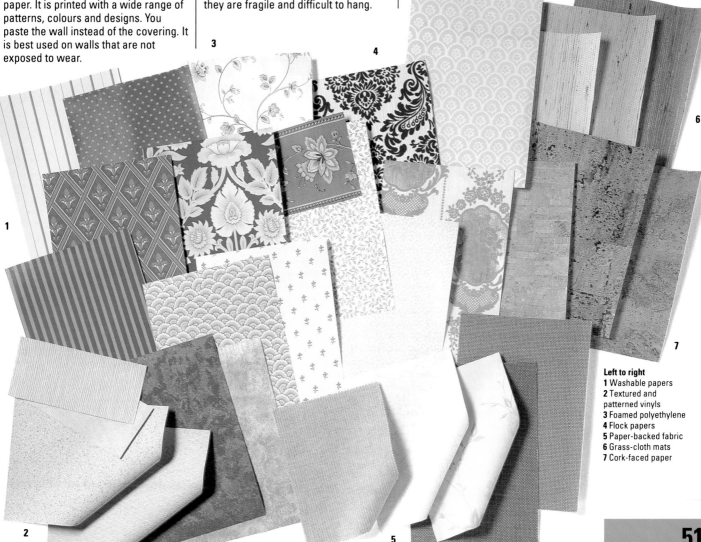

Left to right
1 Washable papers
2 Textured and patterned vinyls
3 Foamed polyethylene
4 Flock papers
5 Paper-backed fabric
6 Grass-cloth mats
7 Cork-faced paper

WALLCOVERINGS: ESTIMATING QUANTITIES

Calculating the number of rolls of wallcovering you will need to cover your walls and ceiling depends on the size of the roll – both length and width – the pattern repeat and the obstructions you have to avoid. Because of variations in colour between batches, you must take into account all these points – and allow for wastage, too. A standard roll of wallcovering measures 520mm (1ft 9in) wide and 10.05 metres (33ft) long. Use the two charts on this page to estimate how many rolls you will need for walls and ceilings.

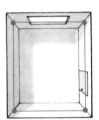

Measuring walls for standard rolls
You can include windows and doors in your estimate.

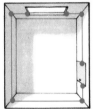

Measuring walls for non-standard rolls
Do not include doors and windows when estimating for expensive materials. Allow for short lengths afterwards.

Estimating non-standard rolls

If the wallcovering is not cut to a standard size, calculate the amount you need in this way:

Walls
Measure the height of the walls from skirting to ceiling. Divide the length of the roll by this figure to find the number of wall lengths you can cut from a roll.

Measure around the room, excluding windows and doors, to work out how many widths fit into the total length of the walls. Divide this number by the number of wall lengths you can get from one roll to find how many rolls you need.

Make an allowance for short lengths above doors and under windows.

Ceilings
Measure the length of the room to determine one strip of paper. Work out how many roll widths fit across the room. Multiply the two figures and divide the answer by the length of a roll to find out how many rolls you need. Check for waste and allow for it.

Checking for shading

If rolls of wallcovering are printed in one batch, there should be no problem with colour matching one roll to another. When you buy, look for the batch number printed on the wrapping.

Make a visual check before hanging the covering, especially for hand-printed papers or fabrics. Unroll a short length of each roll and lay them side by side. You may get a better colour match by changing the rolls around, but if colour difference is obvious, ask for a replacement roll.

Walls:
Standard rolls
Measure your room, then look down height column and across wall column to assess number of standard rolls required.

WALLS	HEIGHT OF ROOM IN METRES FROM SKIRTING							
	2–2.25m	2.25–2.5m	2.5–2.75m	2.75–3m	3–3.25m	3.25–3.5m	3.5–3.75m	3.75–4m
	NUMBER OF ROLLS REQUIRED FOR WALLS							
10m	5	5	6	6	7	7	8	8
10.5m	5	6	6	7	7	8	8	9
11m	5	6	7	7	8	8	9	9
11.5m	6	6	7	7	8	8	9	9
12m	6	6	7	8	8	9	9	10
12.5m	6	7	7	8	9	9	10	10
13m	6	7	8	8	9	10	10	10
13.5m	7	7	8	9	9	10	10	11
14m	7	7	8	9	10	10	11	11
14.5m	7	8	8	9	10	10	11	12
15m	7	8	9	9	10	11	12	12
15.5m	7	8	9	9	10	11	12	13
16m	8	8	9	10	11	11	12	13
16.5m	8	9	9	10	11	12	13	13
17m	8	9	10	10	11	12	13	14
17.5m	8	9	10	11	12	13	14	14
18m	9	9	10	11	12	13	14	15
18.5m	9	10	11	12	12	13	14	15
19m	9	10	11	12	13	14	15	16
19.5m	9	10	11	12	13	14	15	16
20m	9	10	11	12	13	14	15	16
20.5m	10	11	12	13	14	15	16	17
21m	10	11	12	13	14	15	16	17
21.5m	10	11	12	13	14	15	17	18
22m	10	11	13	14	15	16	17	18
22.5m	11	12	13	14	15	16	17	18
23m	11	12	13	14	15	17	18	19
23.5m	11	12	13	15	16	17	18	19
24m	11	12	14	15	16	17	18	20
24.5m	11	13	14	15	16	18	19	20
25m	12	13	14	15	17	18	19	20
25.5m	12	13	14	16	17	18	20	21
26m	12	13	15	16	17	19	20	21
26.5m	12	14	15	16	18	19	20	22
27m	13	14	15	17	18	19	21	22
27.5m	13	14	16	17	18	20	21	23
28m	13	14	16	17	19	20	21	23
28.5m	13	15	16	18	19	20	22	23
29m	13	15	16	18	19	21	22	24
29.5m	14	15	17	18	20	21	23	24
30m	14	15	17	18	20	21	23	24

MEASUREMENT IN METRES AROUND WALLS, INCLUDING DOORS AND WINDOWS

Ceilings:
Standard rolls
Measure perimeter of ceiling. Number of standard rolls required are shown next to overall dimensions.

Dimensions
All dimensions are shown in metres (1m = 39in).

CEILINGS: NUMBER OF ROLLS REQUIRED							
Measurement around room	Number of rolls	Measurement around room	Number of rolls	Measurement around room	Number of rolls	Measurement around room	Number of rolls
11m	2	16m	4	21m	6	26m	9
12m	2	17m	4	22m	7	27m	10
13m	3	18m	5	23m	7	28m	10
14m	3	19m	5	24m	8	29m	11
15m	4	20m	5	25m	8	30m	11

PASTING
WALLCOVERINGS

TRIMMING AND CUTTING TECHNIQUES

Most wallcoverings are machine-trimmed to width so that you can butt adjacent lengths accurately. Some hand-printed papers are left untrimmed. These are usually expensive, so don't attempt to trim them yourself: ask the supplier to do this for you.

Cutting plain wallcoverings

Measure the height of the wall at the point where you will hang the first 'drop'. Add an extra 100mm (4in) for trimming top and bottom. Cut several pieces from your first roll to the same length and mark the top of each one.

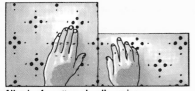

Allowing for patterned wallcoverings
You may have to allow extra on alternate lengths of patterned wallcoverings to match patterns.

CHOOSING PASTE

Most wallpaper pastes are supplied as powder or flakes for mixing with water.

All-purpose paste

Standard wallpaper paste is suitable for most lightweight to medium-weight papers. With less water added, it can be used to hang heavyweight papers.

Heavy-duty paste

Specially prepared to hang embossed papers, paper-backed fabrics and other heavyweight wallcoverings.

Fungicidal paste

Most pastes contain a fungicide to prevent mould growth under impervious wallcoverings such as vinyls, washable papers and foamed-plastic coverings.

Ready-mixed paste

Tubs of ready-mixed, thixotropic paste are specially made for heavyweight wallcoverings such as fabric.

Stain-free paste

For use with delicate papers that could be stained by conventional pastes.

Repair adhesive

Sticks down peeling edges and corners. It even glues vinyl to vinyl.

You can use any wipe-clean table for pasting, but a narrow fold-up pasting table is a good investment if you are doing a lot of decorating. Lay several cut lengths of paper face down on the table to keep it clean. Tuck the ends under a length of string tied loosely round the table legs to stop the paper rolling up while you are pasting.

Applying the paste

Use a large, soft wall brush or pasting brush to apply the paste. Mix the paste in a plastic bucket and tie string across the rim to support the brush, keeping its handle clean while you hang the paper.

Align the wallcovering with the far edge of the table so there will be no paste on the table to be transferred to the face of the wallcovering. Apply the paste by brushing away from the centre. Paste the edges and remove any lumps.

If you prefer, apply the paste with a short-pile paint roller. Pour the paste into a roller tray and roll in one direction only towards the end of the paper.

Pull the covering to the front edge of the table and paste the other half. Fold the pasted end over – don't press it down – and slide the length along the table to expose an unpasted part.

Paste the other end, then fold it over to almost meet the first cut end: the second fold is invariably deeper than the first, a good way to denote the bottom of patterned wallcoverings. Fold long drops concertina-fashion.

Hang vinyls and lightweight papers immediately; drape other coverings over a broom handle spanning two chair backs and leave them to soak. Some heavy or embossed coverings may need to soak for 15 minutes.

Pasting the wall

Hang exotic wallcoverings by pasting the wall instead to reduce the risk of marking their delicate faces. Apply a band of paste just wider than the length of covering, so that you will not have to paste right up to its edge for the next length. Use a brush or roller.

Ready-pasted wallcoverings

Many wallcoverings come precoated with adhesive, activated by soaking a cut length in a trough of cold water. Mix ordinary paste to recoat dry edges.

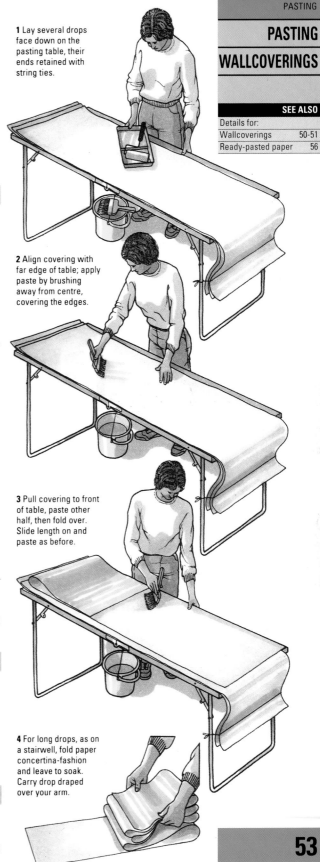

1 Lay several drops face down on the pasting table, their ends retained with string ties.

2 Align covering with far edge of table; apply paste by brushing away from centre, covering the edges.

3 Pull covering to front of table, paste other half, then fold over. Slide length on and paste as before.

4 For long drops, as on a stairwell, fold paper concertina-fashion and leave to soak. Carry drop draped over your arm.

53

PAPERING A WALL

● **Hide a join in a corner**
When you are using a wallcovering with a large pattern, try to finish where it will not be noticeable if the pattern does not quite match.

Sticking down the edges
Ensure that the edges of the paper adhere firmly by running a seam roller along the butt joint.

Losing air bubbles
Slight blistering usually flattens out as wet paper dries and shrinks slightly. If you find that a blister remains, either inject a little paste through it and roll it flat, or cut across it in two directions, peel back the triangular flaps and paste them down.

LINING A WALL

Lining a wall prior to decorating is only necessary if you are hanging embossed or luxury wallcoverings, or if the wall has imperfections that might show through a thin paper. Hang lining paper horizontally so that the joints cannot align with those in the top layer. Work from right to left if you are right-handed and vice versa.

Mark a horizontal line near the top of the wall, one roll-width from the ceiling. Holding the concertina-folded length in one hand, start at the top right-hand corner of the wall, aligning the bottom edge with the marked line. Smooth the paper onto the wall with a paperhanger's brush, working from the centre towards the edges.

Work along the wall gradually, unfolding the length as you do so. Take care not to stretch or tear the wet paper. Use the brush to gently stipple the edge into the corner at each end.

Use the point of a pair of scissors to lightly mark the corner, peel back the paper and trim to the line. Brush the paper back in place. You may have to perform a similar operation along the ceiling if the paper overlaps slightly. Work down the wall butting each strip against the last, or leave a tiny gap between the lengths.

Trim the bottom length to the skirting. Leave the lining paper to dry out for 24 hours before covering.

Lining prior to painting
If you line a wall for emulsion painting, hang the lining paper vertically as you would with other wallcoverings as the joints will hardly show.

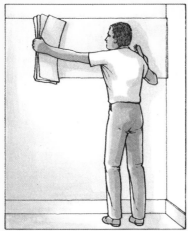

Hanging lining paper horizontally
Hold the concertina-folded paper in one hand and smooth onto the wall from top right, butting strips.

Don't apply any type of wallcovering until all the woodwork has been painted or varnished and the ceiling has been painted or papered.

The traditional method for papering a room is to hang the first length next to a window close to a corner, then work in both directions away from the light, but you may find it easier to paper the longest uninterrupted wall to get used

Centre a large motif over fireplace

Hanging on a straight wall

The walls of an average room are rarely truly square, so use a plumb line to mark a vertical guide against which to hang the first length of wallcovering. Start at one end of the wall and mark the vertical line one roll-width away from the corner, minus 12mm (½in) so the first length will overlap the adjacent wall.

Allowing enough wallcovering for trimming at the ceiling, unfold the top section of the pasted length and hold it against the plumbed line. Using a paperhanger's brush, work gently out from the centre in all directions to squeeze out any trapped air.

When you are sure the paper is positioned accurately, lightly draw the point of your scissors along the ceiling line, peel back the top edge and cut along the crease. Smooth the paper back and stipple it down with the brush. Unpeel the lower fold of the paper, smooth it onto the wall with the brush, then stipple it into the corner. Crease the bottom edge against the skirting, peel away the paper, then trim and brush it back against the wall.

Hang the next length in the same manner. Slide it with your fingertips to align the pattern and produce a perfect butt joint. Wipe any paste from the surface with a damp cloth. Continue to the other side of the wall, allowing the last drop to overlap the adjoining wall by 12mm (½in).

to the basic techniques before tackling corners or obstructions.

If your wallcovering has a large regular motif, centre the first length over the fireplace for symmetry. You could also centre this first length between two windows, unless you will be left with narrow strips each side, in which case it's best to butt two lengths on the centre line.

Butt two lengths between windows

1 Mark first length
Use a roll of paper to mark the wall one width away from the corner – less 12mm (½in) for an overlap onto the return wall – then draw a line from ceiling to skirting, using a plumb line.

2 Hang the first drop
Cut the first drop of paper, allowing about 50mm (2in) at each end for trimming, paste and allow to soak. Hang the top section against the plumbed line and brush out from the centre, working down.

3 Trim at ceiling
When the paper is smoothly brushed on, run the tip of your scissors along the ceiling angle, peel away the paper, cut off the excess, then brush back onto the wall.

4 Trim at skirting
Unfold the lower section of paper. At the skirting, tap your brush into the top edge, peel away the paper and cut along the folded line, then brush back.

Papering around doors and windows

Hang the length next to a door frame, brushing down the butt joint to align the pattern and allowing the other edge to loosely overlap the door.

Make a diagonal cut in the excess towards the top corner of the frame (1). Crease the waste down the side of the frame with scissors, peel it back, trim off then brush back. Leave a 12mm (½in) strip for turning on the top of the frame. Fill in with short strips above the door.

Butt the next full length over the door and cut the excess diagonally into the frame so that you can paste the rest of the strip down the other side of the door. Mark and cut off the waste.

When papering up to flush window frames, treat them like a door. Where a window is set into a reveal, hang the

length of wallcovering next to the window and allow it to overhang the opening. Make a horizontal cut just above the edge of the window reveal. Make a similar cut near the bottom, then fold the paper around to cover the side of the reveal. Crease and trim along the window frame and sill.

Cut a strip of paper to match the width and pattern of the overhang above the window reveal. Paste it, slip it under the overhang and fold it around the top of the reveal (2). Cut through the overlap with a smooth, wavy stroke, remove the excess paper and roll down the joint (3).

To continue, hang short lengths on the wall below and above the window, wrapping top lengths into the reveal.

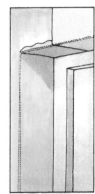

1 Cut the overlap diagonally into the frame

Papering around a fireplace

Paper around a fireplace as for a door. Make a diagonal cut in the waste overlapping the fireplace, up to the edge of the mantel shelf, so that you can tuck the paper in all round for creasing and trimming to the surround.

To cut to an ornate surround, paper

the wall above the surround. Cut strips to fit under the mantel at each side, turning them around the corners of the chimney breast. Gently press the wallcovering into the moulding, peel it away and cut round the impression with nail scissors. Brush the paper back.

2 Fold onto reveal top   **3 Cut with wavy line**

Papering internal and external corners

Turn an internal corner by marking another plumbed line so that the next length of paper covers the overlap from the first wall. If the piece you trimmed off at the corner is wide enough, use it as your first length on the new wall.

To turn an external corner, trim the last length so that it wraps around it, lapping the next wall by about 25mm (1in). Plumb and hang the remaining strip with its edge about 12mm (½in) from the corner.

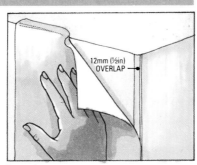

12mm (½in) OVERLAP

Internal corner

25mm (1in) OVERLAP

12mm (½in) FROM CORNER

External corner

- **Papering archways**
Arrange strips to leave even gaps between arch sides and the next full-length strips. Hang strips over face of arch, cut curve leaving 25mm (1in) margin. Fold it onto underside, snipping into margin to prevent creasing. Fit a strip on the underside to reach from floor to top of arch. Repeat on opposite side of arch.

Papering behind radiators

If you cannot remove a radiator, turn off the heating and allow it to cool. Use a steel tape to measure the positions of the brackets along the radiator to the wall. Transfer these measurements to a length of wallcovering and slit it from

the bottom to the top of the bracket. Feed the pasted paper behind the radiator, down both sides of the brackets. Use a radiator roller to press it to the wall. Crease and trim to the skirting board.

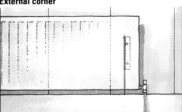

Slit to top of bracket behind radiator

Papering around switches and sockets

Turn off the electricity at the mains. Hang the wallcovering over the switch or socket. Make diagonal cuts from the centre of the fitting to each corner and tap the excess paper against the edges

of the faceplate with the brush. Trim off the waste, leaving 6mm (¼in) all round. Loosen the faceplate, tuck the margin behind and retighten it. Don't switch the power back on until the paste is dry.

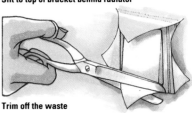

Trim off the waste

STAIRWELLS

The only real problem with papering a stairwell is having to handle the extra-long drops on the side walls. You will need to build a safe work platform over the stairs. Plumb and hang the longest drop first, lapping the head wall above the stairs by 12mm (½in).

Carrying the long drops of wallcovering – sometimes as much as 4.5m (15ft) long – is awkward: paste the covering liberally so that it's not likely to dry out while you hang it, then fold it concertina-fashion. Drape it over your arm while you climb the platform. You will need an assistant to support the weight of the pasted length while you apply it. Unfold the flaps as you work down the wall.

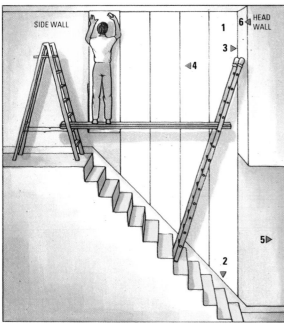

SIDE WALL

HEAD WALL

Papering sequence
Follow the sequence for papering a stairwell.
1 Hang the longest drop.
2 Crease it into the angled skirting and trim to fit.
3 Lap the paper onto the head wall.
4 & 5 Work away from the first drop in both directions.
6 Paper the head wall.

Crease and cut the bottom of the paper against the angled skirting. Don't forget to allow for this angle when first you cut the length; work to the longest edge measurement. Work away from this first length in both directions, then paper the head wall.

Where the banister rail is let into the stairwell wall, try to arrange the rolls so that the rail falls between two butted drops. Hang the drops to the rail and cut horizontally into the edge of the last strip at the centre of the rail, then make radial cuts so the paper can be moulded around the rail. Crease the flaps, peel away the wallcovering and cut them off. Smooth the covering back.

Hang the next drop at the other side of the rail, butting it to the previous piece, and make similar radial cuts.

SPECIAL TECHNIQUES FOR WALLPAPERING

No matter what kind of wallcovering you may be using, the standard wallpapering techniques previously explained hold good. However, there are some additional considerations and special techniques involved in applying some types of covering.

Relief wallcoverings

When hanging embossed-paper wallcoverings, line the wall first and use a heavy-duty paste. Apply the paste liberally and evenly, but try not to leave too much paste in the depressions. Allow it to soak for 10 minutes (or, for cotton-fibre wallcoverings, 15 minutes) before you hang it.

Don't use a seam roller on the butt joints. Instead, tap the paper down with a paperhanger's brush to avoid flattening the pattern.

Don't turn a relief wallcovering around corners. Measure the distance from the last drop to the corner and cut your next length to fit. Trim and hang the offcut to meet at the corner. Fill external corners with cellulose filler once the paper has dried thoroughly.

Lincrusta is available in a limited range of original Victorian patterns for re-creating period-style decorative schemes. Hanging this expensive material requires special techniques that are difficult to master, and it pays in the long run to leave it to an expert.

Vinyl wallcoverings

Paste paper-backed vinyls in the normal way. Cotton-backed vinyl hangs better if you paste the wall and then leave it to become tacky before you apply the wallcovering. Use fungicidal paste.

Hang and butt-join lengths of vinyl, using a sponge to smooth them onto the wall rather than a brush. Crease a length top and bottom, then trim it to size with a sharp knife.

Vinyl will not normally stick to itself, so when you turn a corner use a knife to cut through both pieces of paper where they overlap. Peel away the excess and rub down the vinyl to produce a perfect butt joint. Alternatively, glue the overlap, using a tube of repair adhesive.

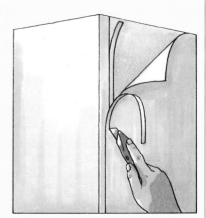

Cut through overlap and remove excess

Ready-pasted wallcoverings

Place the trough of cold water next to the skirting at the position of the first drop. Roll a cut length loosely from the outside. Immerse the roll in the trough for the prescribed time, according to the manufacturer's instructions.

Take hold of the cut end and lift the paper, allowing it to unroll naturally and draining the surface water back into the trough at the same time. Hang and butt-join in the usual way, using a sponge to apply vinyls and a paperhanger's brush for other coverings.

Hanging a long wet length can be difficult if you follow the standard procedure. Instead, roll the length from the top with the pattern outermost. Place it in the trough and immediately reroll it through the water. Take it from the trough in roll form and drain excess water, then unroll the strip as you proceed to hang it.

Pull paper from trough and hang on the wall

SPECIAL TECHNIQUES FOR WALLPAPERING

Foamed polyethylene

A foamed-plastic wallcovering can be hung straight from the roll onto a pasted wall. Sponge in place and trim it top and bottom with scissors.

Flock paper

Protect the flocking with a piece of lining paper as you remove air bubbles with a paperhanger's brush. Cut through both thicknesses of overlapping strips and remove the surplus; press back the edges to make a neat butt joint.

Fabrics and special coverings

Try to keep paste off the face of paper-backed fabrics and any other special wallcoverings. There are many different types of wallcovering, so check with the supplier which paste to use for the one you have chosen.

In order to avoid damaging a delicate surface, use a felt or rubber roller to press the covering in place or stipple gently with a brush.

Most fabric coverings will be machine-trimmed, but if the edges are frayed, overlap the joints and cut through both thicknesses, then peel off the waste to make a butt joint. Make a similar joint at a corner.

Many fabrics are sold in wide rolls: even one cut length will be heavy and awkward to handle. Paste the wall, then support the rolled length on a batten between two stepladders. Work from the bottom upwards.

PASTE WALL

BATTEN SUPPORT

FABRIC ROLL

Supporting heavy fabric

Expanded polystyrene

Paint or roll special ready-mixed adhesive onto the wall. Hang the covering straight from the roll, smooth gently with the flat of your hand, then roll over it lightly with a dry paint roller.

If the edge is square, butt adjacent drops. If it is crushed or crumbled, overlap the join and cut through both thicknesses with a sharp trimming knife, peel away the offcuts and rub the edges down. Unless the edges are generously glued, they will curl apart. Trim top and bottom with a knife and straightedge. Allow to dry for 72 hours, then hang a subsequent wallcovering using a thick fungicidal paste.

Hang the wallcovering straight from the roll

If you want to apply a plain-coloured medium-weight fabric, you can glue it directly to the wall. However, it can be difficult to align a pattern if the fabric stretches.

For more control, stretch the fabric onto 12mm (½in) thick panels of lightweight insulation board (you will then have the added advantage of insulation and a pin-board). Stick the boards directly onto the wall.

Using paste

Test an offcut of fabric to make sure the adhesive will not stain it. Use a ready-mixed paste and roll it onto the wall.

Wrap a cut length of fabric around a cardboard tube (from a carpet supplier) and gradually unroll it on the surface, smoothing it down with a dry paint roller. Take care not to distort the weave. Overlap the joins, but do not cut through them until the paste has dried in case the fabric shrinks. Reapply paste and close the seam.

Press the fabric into the ceiling line and skirting, then trim away the excess with a sharp trimming knife when the paste has set.

Making wall panels

Cut the insulation board to suit the width of the fabric and the height of the wall. Stretch the fabric across the panel, wrap it around the edges, then use latex adhesive to stick it to the back. Hold it temporarily with drawing pins while the adhesive dries.

Either use wallboard adhesive to glue the panels to the wall or pin them, tapping the nail heads through the weave of the fabric to conceal them.

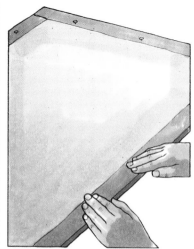

Stretch unbacked fabric over insulation board

57

PAPERING A CEILING

Papering a ceiling isn't as difficult as you may think: the techniques are basically the same as for papering a wall, except that the drops are usually longer and more unwieldy to hold while you brush the paper into place. Set up a sensible work platform – it's virtually impossible to work from a single stepladder – and enlist a helper to support the folded paper while you position one end, progressing backwards across the room. If you have marked out the ceiling first, the result should be faultless.

Setting out the ceiling

Arrange your work platform before you begin to plan out the papering sequence for the ceiling. The best type of platform to use is a purpose-made decorator's trestle, but you can manage with a pair of scaffold boards spanning two stepladders.

Now mark the ceiling to give a visual guide to positioning the strips of paper. Aim to work parallel with the window wall and away from the light, so you can see what you are doing and so that the light will not highlight the joints between strips. If the distance is shorter the other way, hang the strips in that direction for ease.

Mark a guideline along the ceiling, one roll-width minus 12mm (½in) from the side wall, so that the first strip of paper will lap onto the wall.

Putting up the paper

Paste the paper as for a wallcovering and fold it concertina-fashion. Drape the folded length over a spare roll and carry it to the work platform. You will find it easier if a helper supports the folded paper, leaving both your hands free for brushing it into place.

Hold the strip against the guideline, using a brush to stroke it onto the ceiling. Tap it into the wall angle, then gradually work backwards along the

scaffold board, brushing on the paper as your helper unfolds it.

If the ceiling has a cornice, crease and trim the paper at the ends. Otherwise, leave it to lap the walls by 12mm (½in) so that it will be covered by the wallcovering. Work across the ceiling in the same way, butting the lengths of paper together. Cut the final strip roughly to width, and trim into the wall angle.

Working from a ladder
If you have to work from a stepladder, an assistant can support the paper on a cardboard tube taped to a broom.

Papering a ceiling
The job is much easier if two people work together.
1 Mark a guideline on the ceiling.
2 Support the folded paper on a tube.
3 Brush on the paper from the centre outwards.
4 The overlap is eventually covered by wallpaper.
5 Use a pair of boards to support two people.

LIGHTING FITTINGS AND CENTREPIECES

Unlike walls, where you have doors, windows and radiators to contend with, there are few obstructions on a ceiling to make papering difficult. The only problem areas occur where there is a pendant light fitting or a decorative plaster centrepiece.

Cutting around a pendant light
Where the paper passes over a ceiling rose, cut several triangular flaps so that you can pass the light fitting through the hole. Tap the paper all round the rose with a paperhanger's brush and continue on to the end of the length. Return to the rose and cut off the flaps with a knife.

Papering around a centrepiece
If you have a decorative plaster centrepiece, work out the position of the strips so that a joint will pass through the middle. Cut long flaps from the side of each piece so that you can tuck it in all round the plaster moulding.

Cut off triangular flaps when paste is dry

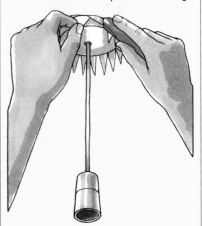

Cut long strips to fit around moulding

Tiling is a popular method of decorating a surface, with an almost inexhaustible range of colours, textures and patterns to choose from depending on the degree of durability required. Tiling provides the facility of finishing a surface with small, regular units which can be cut and fitted into an awkward shape far more easily than can sheet materials.

Glazed ceramic tiles
Hard ceramic tiles, usually glazed and fired, are made for walls and floors. Unglazed tiles are available to provide a surer grip for flooring; a textured surface reduces the risk of accidents where a floor might become wet. All ceramic tiles are durable and waterproof but, where appropriate, be sure to use special tiles that are resistant to heat or frost. Do not use wall tiles on the floor as they cannot take the weight of traffic or furniture.

The majority of tiles are square, the dimensions varying according to use and the manufacturer's preference. Rectangular and more irregularly shaped tiles are also available: typical shapes include hexagons, octagons, diamonds and interlocking units with curved, elaborate edges, as well as slim rectangles with either pointed (pic) or slanted (cane) ends. Use them in combination to produce patterned floors and walls.

Mosaic tiles
Mosaic tiles are small versions of the standard ceramic tiles. To lay them individually would be time-consuming and lead to inaccuracy, so they are usually joined by a paper covering, or a mesh background, into larger panels. Square tiles are common, but rectangular, hexagonal and round mosaics are also available. Because they are small, mosaics can be used on curved surfaces, and will fit irregular shapes better than large ceramic tiles.

Quarry tiles
Quarry tiles are thick, unglazed ceramic tiles which are used for floors which need a hardwearing, waterproof surface. The colours are limited to browns, reds, black and white. Machine-made tiles are regular in size and even in colour but hand-made ones are variable, producing a beautiful mottled effect. Quarry tiles are difficult to cut, so do not contemplate using them where you will have to try to fit them against a complicated shape. Round-edge quarry tiles can be used as treads for steps, and skirting tiles are available for finishing a floor.

Stone and slate flooring
A floor laid with real stone or slate tiles will be exquisite but expensive. Sizes and thicknesses vary according to the manufacturer – some will even cut to measure. A few materials are so costly that you should consider hiring a professional to lay them, otherwise treat cheaper ones like quarry tiles.

SEE ALSO

Details for:	
Choosing colour/ pattern	6-7, 11
Preparing plaster	22-23
Wall tiling	62-64
Floor tiling	67–71

Standard tile sections
A range of sections is produced for specific functions:

Field tile for general tiling with spacing lugs moulded onto it.

Rounded-edge (RE) tile for edging the field.

REX tile with two adjacent rounded edges.

Universal tile with two glazed, square edges for use in any position.

Tile selection
The examples shown left are a typical cross-section of commercially available ceramic tiles.
1 Glazed ceramic
2 Shape and size variation
3 Mosaic tiles
4 Quarry tiles
5 Slate and stone

CHOOSING
TILES

Stone and brick tiles

Thin masonry facing tiles can be used to simulate a stone or brick wall as a feature area for a chimney breast, for example, or to clad a whole wall. Stone tiles are typically made from reconstituted stone in moulds, and most look unconvincing as an imitation of the real thing. Colour choice is intended to reflect local stone types, and is typically white, grey or buff. Some 'weathered' versions are also made.

Brick tiles look much more authentic. The best ones are actually brick 'slips' – slivers cut from kiln-produced bricks. A very wide range of traditional brick colours is available.

Brick tiles
For the best result, use fired-clay slips.

Carpet tiles

Carpet tiles have advantages over wall-to-wall carpeting. An error is less crucial when cutting a single tile to fit, and, being loose-laid, a worn, burnt or stained tile can be replaced instantly. However, you can't substitute a brand-new tile several years later, as the colour will not match. Buy several spares initially and swap them around regularly to even out the wear and colour change. Most types of carpet are available as tiles, including cord, loop and twist piles in wool as well as a range of man-made fibres. Tiles are normally plain in colour, but some are patterned to give a grid effect. Some tiles have an integral rubber underlay.

Carpet tiles make hardwearing floorcoverings

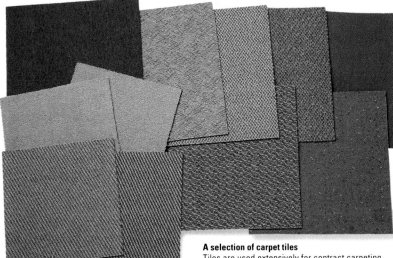

A selection of carpet tiles
Tiles are used extensively for contract carpeting, but they are equally suitable as a hardwearing floorcovering in the home.

Vinyl tiles

Vinyl tiles are among the cheapest and easiest floorcoverings to use. Vinyl can be cut easily, and provided the tiles are firmly glued, with good joints, the floor will be waterproof. However, it will still be susceptible to scorching. A standard coated tile has a printed pattern between a vinyl backing and a harder, clear-vinyl surface. Solid-vinyl tiles are made entirely of the hardwearing plastic. Some vinyl tiles have a high proportion of mineral filler. As a result they are stiff and must be laid on a perfectly flat base. Unlike standard vinyl tiles, they will resist some rising damp in a concrete sub-floor. Most tiles are square or rectangular, but there are interlocking shapes and hexagons. There are many patterns and colours to choose from, including embossed vinyl which represents ceramic, brick or stone tiling.

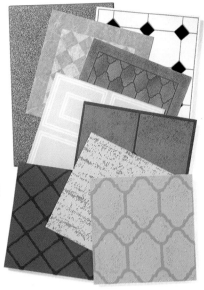

Vinyl tiles can simulate other flooring materials

1

Polystyrene tiles
Although expanded-polystyrene tiles will not reduce heat loss from a room by any significant amount, they will prevent condensation as well as mask a ceiling in poor condition. Polystyrene cuts easily provided the trimming knife is very sharp. For safety in case of fire, choose a self-extinguishing type and do not overpaint with an oil paint. Wall tiles are made, but they will crush easily and are not suitable for use in a vulnerable area. Polystyrene tiles may be flat or decoratively embossed.

Mineral-fibre tiles
Ceiling tiles made from compressed mineral fibre are dense enough to be sound-insulating and heat-insulating. They are normally fitted into a suspended grid system that may be exposed or concealed depending on whether the tile edges are rebated or grooved. Fibre tiles can also be glued directly to a flat ceiling. A range of textured surfaces is available.

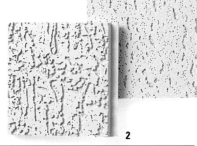
2

Mirror tiles
Square and rectangular mirror tiles are attached to walls by means of a self-adhesive pad in each corner. There is a choice of silver or bronze finish. Don't expect these tiles to produce a perfect reflection unless they are mounted on a completely flat surface.

Plastic tiles
Insulated plastic wall tiles inhibit condensation. Provided you don't use abrasive cleaners on them they are relatively durable, but they will melt if subjected to direct heat. A special grout is applied to fill the 'joints' moulded across the 300mm (1ft) square tiles.

3

4

Rubber tiles
Rubber tiles were originally made for use in shops and offices, but they are equally suitable for the home, being hardwearing yet soft and quiet to walk on. The surface is usually studded or textured to improve the grip.

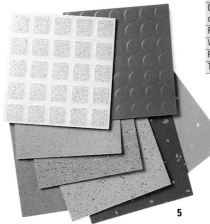
5

Cork tiles
Cork is a popular covering for walls and floors. It is easy to lay with contact adhesive and can be cut to size and shape with a knife. A wide range of textures and warm colours is available. Presanded but unfinished cork will darken in tone when you varnish it. Alternatively, you can buy ready-finished tiles with various plastic and wax coatings. Soft, granular insulating cork is suitable as a decorative finish for walls only. It crumbles easily, so should not be used where it will be exposed on external corners.

6

Left to right
1 Polystyrene tiles
2 Mineral-fibre tiles
3 Mirror tiles
4 Plastic tiles
5 Rubber tiles
6 Cork floor tiles

61

SETTING OUT
FOR WALL TILES

Setting out
The setting-out procedure described on this page is applicable to the following tiles: cork, mosaics, ceramic, mirror and plastic.

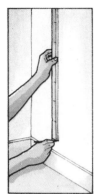

Using a gauge stick
Hold a home-made gauge stick firmly against the wall and mark the positions of the tiles on the surface.

Setting out for tiling
Plan different arrangements of wall tiles as shown right, but first plot the symmetry of the tile field with a gauge stick to ensure a wide margin all round.
1 Temporarily fix a horizontal batten at the base of the field.
2 Mark the centre of the wall.
3 Gauge from the mark, then fix a vertical batten to indicate the side of the field.
4 Start under a dado rail with whole tiles.
5 Use a row of whole tiles at sill level.
6 Place cut tiles at back of a reveal.
7 Support tiles over window while they set.

Whatever type of tiles you plan to use, the walls must be clean, sound and dry. You cannot tile over wallpaper, and flaking or powdery paint must be treated first to give a suitable stable base for the tiles. It is important that you make the surface as flat as possible so the tiles will stick firmly. Setting out the prepared surface accurately is vital to hanging the tiles properly.

MAKING A GAUGE STICK

First make a gauge stick (a tool for plotting the position of tiles on the wall) from a length of 50 x12mm (2 x ½in) softwood. Lay several tiles along it, butting together those with lugs, or add spacers for square-edged tiles, unless they are intended to be close-butted. Mark the position of each tile on the softwood batten.

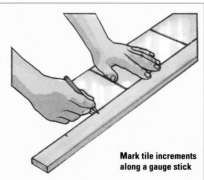

Mark tile increments along a gauge stick

Setting out a plain wall

On a plain uninterrupted wall, use the gauge stick to plan horizontal rows starting at skirting level. If you are left with a narrow strip at the top, move the rows up half a tile-width to create a wider margin. Mark the bottom of the lowest row of whole tiles. Temporarily nail a thin guide batten to the wall aligned with the mark (**1**). Make sure it is horizontal by placing a level on top.

Mark the centre of the wall (**2**), then use the gauge stick to set out the vertical rows at each side of it. If the border tiles measure less than half a width, reposition the rows sideways by half a tile. Use a spirit level to position a guide batten against the last vertical line and nail it to the wall (**3**).

Plotting a half-tiled wall

If you are tiling part of a wall only (up to a dado rail, for example) set out the tiles with a row of whole tiles at the top (**4**).

This is even more important if you are using RE tiles which are used for the top row of a half-tiled wall.

Arranging tiles around a window

Use a window as your starting point so that the tiles surrounding it are equal in size, but not too narrow. If possible, begin a row of whole tiles at sill level

(**5**), and position cut tiles at the back of a window reveal (**6**). Fix a guide batten over a window to support a row of tiles temporarily (**7**).

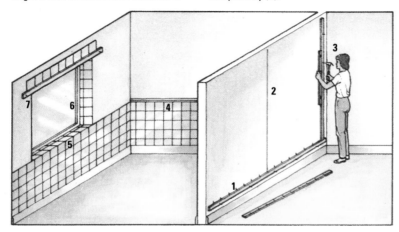

RENOVATING TILES

A properly tiled surface should last for many years, but the appearance is often spoiled by one or two damaged tiles (particularly the lifting of cork, vinyl or polystyrene tiles) and by discoloured grouting between ceramic tiles. There is usually no need to redecorate as most problems can be solved fairly easily.

Renewing the grouting
It's not necessary to rake out old, drab grouting: use a renovator to brighten it up instead. This liquid colourant forms a water-resistant bond with grout but does not adhere to ceramic surfaces. Wash the tiles with sugar soap and let them dry overnight. Paint the renovator along the joints and leave it to dry for a couple of hours. Wet the whole tiling with a plant spray and after three minutes wipe off excess colourant with a damp sponge. Dry and polish the tiles with a soft cloth or paper towel.

Replacing a cracked ceramic tile
Scrape the grout from the damaged tile, then use a fine cold chisel to chip out the tile, working from the centre. Take care not to dislodge its neighbours.
Scrape out the remains of the adhesive and vacuum the recess. Butter the back of the replacement tile with adhesive, then press it firmly in place. Wipe off excess adhesive, allow it to set, then renew the grouting.

Lifting a cork or vinyl floor tile
Try to remove a single tile by chopping it out from the centre with a wood chisel. If the adhesive is firm, warm the tile with a domestic iron (or a hot-air gun on a very low setting, but take care not to damage the surrounding tiles). Scrape the old adhesive from the floor and try the new tile for fit. Trim it if necessary. Spread adhesive on the floor, then place one corner of the tile in position. Gradually lower the tile into place, then press with your fingertips to squeeze out any air bubbles, place a heavy weight on it and leave overnight.

Removing a ceiling tile
Loosen a polystyrene tile by picking it out from the centre with a sharp knife and paint scraper. Don't lever it out or you will crush the adjoining tile. Stick the replacement tile on a complete bed of special adhesive. Remove a stapled ceiling tile by cutting through the tongues all round.

TILING A WALL:
CERAMIC TILES

Choosing the correct adhesive

Most ceramic-tile adhesives are sold ready-mixed, although a few need to be mixed with water. The tubs or packets will state the coverage.

A standard adhesive is suitable for most applications, but use a waterproof type in areas likely to be subjected to running water or splashing. If the tiles are to be laid on a wallboard, use a flexible adhesive and make sure that it is heat-resistant if you are tiling above worktops or around a fireplace. Some adhesives can also be used for grouting the finished wall. A notched plastic spreader is usually supplied with each tub, or you can use a serrated trowel.

Hanging the tiles

Spread enough adhesive on the wall to cover about 1 metre square (about 3ft 3 in square). Press the teeth of the spreader against the surface and drag it through the adhesive so that it forms horizontal ridges (**1**).

Press the first tile into the angle formed by the setting out battens (**2**) until it is firmly fixed, then butt up tiles on each side. Build up three or four rows at a time. If the tiles do not have lugs, place proprietary plastic spacers between them to form the grout lines.

Wipe away adhesive from the surface with a damp sponge.

Spread more adhesive, and tile along the batten until the first rows of whole tiles are complete. From time to time, check that your tiling is accurate by holding a batten and spirit level across the faces and along the top and side edges. When you have completed the entire field, scrape adhesive from the border and allow the rest to set before removing the setting-out battens and proceeding with the grouting.

Grouting tiles and sealing joins

Use a ready-mixed paste called grout to fill the gaps between the tiles. Standard grouts are white, grey or brown, but there is also a range of coloured grouts to match or contrast with the tiles. Alternatively, to match a particular colour, mix pigments with dry, powdered grout before adding water.

Waterproof grout is essential for showers and bath surrounds, and you should use an epoxy-based grout for worktops to keep them germ-free.

Leave the adhesive to harden for 24 hours, then use a rubber-bladed spreader to press the grout into the joints (**3**). Spread it in all directions to make sure all joints are well filled.

Wipe grout from the surface of the tiles with a sponge before it sets and smooth the joints with a blunt-ended stick – a sharpened dowel will do. When the grout has dried, polish the tiles with a dry cloth.

Do not use a tiled shower for about seven days to make sure the grout hardens thoroughly.

Sealing around bathroom fittings

Don't use grout or ordinary filler to seal the gap between a tiled wall and shower tray, bath or basin: the fittings can flex enough to crack a rigid seal, and frequent soakings will allow water to seep in, create stains and damage the floor and wall. Use a silicone-rubber caulking compound to fill the gaps; it remains flexible enough to accommodate any movement.

Packed in cartridges, sealants are available in a choice of colours to match popular tile and sanitaryware colourways. They can cope with gaps up to 3mm (⅛in) wide. Alternatively, use a strip of press-in-place sealant.

If you are using a cartridge, trim the end off the plastic nozzle (the amount you cut off dictates the thickness of the bead) and press the tip into the joint at an angle of 45 degrees. Push forward at a steady rate while squeezing the applicator's trigger or the base of the cartridge itself to apply a bead of sealant (**4**). Smooth any ripples with the back of a wetted teaspoon.

Ceramic coving or quadrant tiles are made for edging a bath or shower unit, and there are glue-on plastic coving strips which you cut to length.

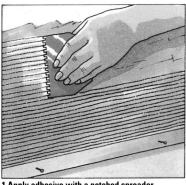

1 Apply adhesive with a notched spreader

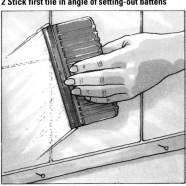

2 Stick first tile in angle of setting-out battens

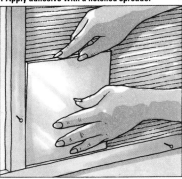

3 Press grout into joints with rubber spreader

4 Seal between tiles and fittings with sealant

Ceramic coving tiles

Quadrant
Used to fill the joint between bath and wall.

Mitred tile
Use at the end if you want to turn a corner.

Bullnose tile
Use this tile to finish the end of a straight run.

● **Tiling around pipes and fittings**
Check with the gauge stick how the tiles will fit round socket outlets and switches, pipes and other obstructions. Make slight adjustments to the position of the main field to avoid difficult shaping around these features.

CUTTING CERAMIC TILES

Tile-cutting jig
A worthwhile investment if you are cutting a lot of tiles, a proprietary jig incorporates a device for measuring and scoring tiles. A cutter is drawn down the channel of the adjustable guide. The tile is then snapped with a special pincer-action tool.

Having finished a main field of tiles you will have to cut ceramic tiles to fill the borders and to fit around obstructions such as window frames, electrical fittings, pipes and a basin. Protect your eyes with safety spectacles or goggles when snapping scored ceramic tiles.

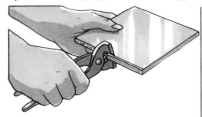

Cutting thin strips
A cutting jig is the most accurate tool for cutting a thin strip cleanly from the edge of a tile. If you do not want to use the strip itself, nibble away the waste a little at a time with pincers or special tile nibblers.

Tiling around a window
Tile up to the edges of a window, then stick RE tiles to the reveal so that they lap the edges of surrounding tiles. Fill in any space left behind the edging tiles with cut tiles.

Cutting a curve
To fit a tile against a curved shape, cut a template from thin card to the exact size of a tile. Cut 'fingers' along one edge; press them against the curve to reproduce the shape. Transfer the curve onto the face of the tile and cut away the waste with a tile saw – a thin rod coated with hard, abrasive particles which will cut in any direction.

Mark two edges   **Cut and fit tile**

Fitting around a pipe
Mark the centre of the pipe on the top and side edges of a tile and draw lines across the tile from these points. Where they cross, draw round a coin or something slightly larger than the diameter of the pipe.

Make one straight cut through the centre of the circle and either nibble out the waste, having scored the curve, or clamp it in a vice, protected with softening, and cut it out with a tile saw. Stick one half of the tile on each side of the pipe.

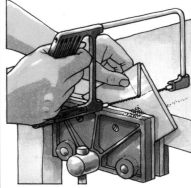

Fitting around a socket or switch
In order to fit around a socket or switch you may have to cut the corner out of a tile. Mark it from the socket, then clamp the tile in a vice, protected with softening. Score both lines, then use a saw file to make one diagonal cut from the corner of the tile to where the lines meet. Snap out both triangles.

If you have to cut a notch out of a large tile, cut down both sides with a hacksaw, then score between them and snap the piece out of the middle.

CUTTING BORDER TILES

It's necessary to cut border tiles one at a time to fit the gap between the field tiles and the adjacent wall: walls are rarely truly square and the margin is bound to be uneven.

Making straight cuts
Mark a border tile by placing it face down over its neighbour with one edge against the adjacent wall (**1**). Make an allowance for normal spacing between the tiles. Transfer the marks to the edge of the tiles using a felt-tip pen.

Use a proprietary tile cutter held against a straightedge to score across the face with one firm stroke to cut through the glaze (**2**). You may also have to score the edges of thick tiles.

Stretch a length of thin wire across a panel of chipboard, place the scored line directly over the wire and press down on both sides to snap the tile (**3**).

If you are planning to do a lot of tiling, it will pay to invest in a purpose-made tile-cutting jig. Inexpensive plastic jigs (see left) are perfectly adequate for relatively thin tiles, but there are also substantial jigs that can cope with tiles of any thickness. These jigs enable you to score tiles accurately and snap them with ease every time.

Smooth the cut edges of the tile with a tile sander or small slipstone.

1 Mark the edge tile

2 Score the marked line

3 Snap the tile over a wire

Mosaic tiles

Ceramic mosaic tiles are applied to a wall in a similar way to large square tiles. Set out the wall and use the same adhesive and grout.

Some mosaics have a mesh backing, which is pressed into the adhesive. Others have facing paper which is left on the surface until the adhesive sets.

Fill the main area of the wall, spacing the sheets to equal the gaps between individual tiles. Place a carpet-covered board over the sheets and tap it with a mallet to bed the tiles into the adhesive.

Fill borders by cutting strips from the sheet. Cut individual tiles to fit awkward shapes around fittings. If necessary, soak off the facing paper with a damp sponge, then grout the tiles.

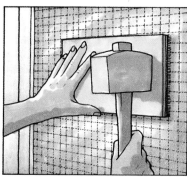

Bedding mosaics
Bed tiles by tapping a carpet-covered board.

Mirror tiles

Avoid using mirror tiles in an area which would entail complicated fitting, as it is difficult to cut glass except in straight lines. Mirror tiles are fixed close-butted with self-adhesive pads. No grout is necessary.

Set out the wall with battens. Peel the protective paper from the pads and lightly position each tile. Check its alignment with a spirit level, then press it firmly into place with a soft cloth.

Use a wooden straightedge and a glass cutter to score a line across a tile. Make one firm stroke. Lay the tile over a stretched wire and press down on both sides. Remove the sharp cut edge with an oiled slipstone.

Add spare pads and fix the tile in place. Finally, polish the tiles to remove any unsightly fingermarks.

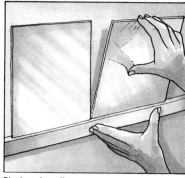

Placing mirror tiles
Position tile before pressing on wall.

Plastic tiles

You can cover a wall relatively quickly with 300mm (1ft) square moulded-plastic tiles. Being backed with expanded polystyrene, the tiles are extremely lightweight and warm to the touch. They are ideal in bathrooms or kitchens where condensation is a problem, but don't hang them in close proximity to cookers, boilers or even radiators – they may soften and distort.

Set out the area to be tiled with guide battens, and spread the special manufacturer's adhesive thinly across the back of each tile. Press the tiles firmly against the wall, butting them together gently. Being flexible, plastic tiles will accommodate slightly imperfect walls.

Grout the moulded 'joints' with the branded non-abrasive product sold with the tiles. Use a damp sponge to remove surplus grout before it sets hard, or employ methylated spirit afterwards.

Plastic tiles are easy to shape with scissors or a craft knife when fitting around pipework or electrical points.

Shaping plastic tiles
Shape insulated plastic tiles with scissors.

Cork tiles

Set up a horizontal guide batten to make sure you lay the tiles accurately. It isn't necessary to fix a vertical batten, however; the large tiles are easy to align without one. Simply mark a vertical line centrally on the wall and hang the tiles in both directions from it.

You will need a rubber-based contact adhesive to fix cork tiles. It pays to use a glue that allows a degree of movement when positioning the tiles. If any adhesive gets onto the surface of a tile, clean it off immediately with a suitable solvent on a cloth.

Spread adhesive thinly and evenly onto the wall and the back of the tiles and leave it to dry. Lay each tile by placing one edge only against the batten or its neighbour, then gradually press the rest of the tile onto the wall.

Smooth it down with your palms.

Cut cork tiles with a sharp trimming knife. Because the edges are butted tightly, you will need to be very accurate when marking out border tiles. Use the same method as for laying cork and vinyl floor tiles. Cut and fit curved shapes using a template.

Unless the tiles are precoated, apply two coats of varnish after 24 hours.

Tiling around curves
In many older houses some walls might be rounded at the external corners. Flexible tiles such as vinyl and rubber are easy to bend into quite tight radii, but cork will snap if bent too far. Cut a series of shallow slits down the back of a cork tile with a tenon saw, then bend the tile gently to the curve required.

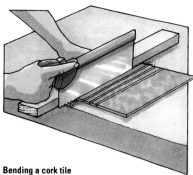

Bending a cork tile
Using a tenon saw, cut a series of shallow slits vertically down the back of a tile, then bend it gently: the slits will enable the tile to assume a fairly tight curve without snapping, but experiment first with a spare tile.

FIXING
BRICK TILES

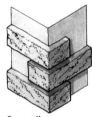

Applying adhesive
Butter the tile back
using a notched
spreader.

Corner tiles
Start with three
preformed corner tiles
at each end of a run.

Fixing brick tiles
Follow this procedure
when fixing brick tiles
to your wall.
1 Plot the tile courses
vertically and
horizontally with two
gauge sticks. Allow
joint spaces between
each tile.
2 Use preformed tiles
at external corners.
3 Set a course of tiles
on end above a
window as a brick
lintel.
4 Set the bottom row
of tiles on the skirting
or substitute with a
row of brick tiles set
on end.
5 Leave a gap for
ventilating the flue in a
blocked-off fireplace.
6 Fix tiles from the
bottom up, staggering
the vertical joints.

Brick tiles can look quite authentic if they are laid in any of the standard
brick-bond patterns, especially if you point them carefully with mortar.
You can either leave the skirting in place and start the first course of
tiles just above it, or remove the skirting and replace it just lapping over
the bottom course of tiles for an authentic appearance. Alternatively,
remove the skirting and set a row of brick tiles on end.

Setting out the wall

Make two gauge sticks, one for the
vertical coursing and another to space
the tiles sideways. Allow 10mm (⅜in)
spacing between each tile for the
mortar joints, but adjust this slightly if
need be so there will be a full-width tile
top and bottom.

Work out your spacing side to side
so that, if possible, you have one course
of whole tiles, alternating with courses
containing a half tile at each end.

If you are using corner tiles at each
end, work out your spacing from them
towards the middle of a wall, and place
cut tiles centrally.

Fitting around a window
Lay tiles vertically above a window in a
'soldier course' to simulate a brick
lintel. Use prefabricated corner tiles to
take the brickwork into a window reveal
for the most realistic effect.

Cutting brick tiles
Most brick tiles can be cut with a
hacksaw, but if a cut edge looks too
sharp, round it over by rubbing with a
scrap piece of tile. You can also cut
tiles using a club hammer and bolster
chisel; the thinnest type can even be
cut with scissors.

Gluing on the tiles

You can use mortar to stick brick tiles to
the wall, but most types are sold with a
compatible adhesive. Use a notched
spreader to coat the back of each tile,
then press it on the wall. (Some
manufacturers recommend spreading
the adhesive onto the wall rather than
the tile – check instructions.)

If you are using preformed corner
tiles, fix them first, three at a time,
alternating headers and stretchers to
resemble real brickwork. Using a batten
and spirit level, check that they are
level at each side of the wall.

Fill in one row at a time, using small
10mm (⅜in) wooden offcuts to space
the tiles: alternatively, the polystyrene
packing that comes with some tiles can
be cut into pieces to use as spacers.
Every third course, check the alignment
of the tiles with a spirit level and adjust
them if necessary.

Pointing the joints
After 24 hours, use a ready-mixed
mortar to point the wall as if it were real
brickwork. Brush mortar from the face
of the tiles with a stiff-bristle brush.

STONE TILES

Stone tiles are laid in the same way as
brick tiles. Coursed stones should be
arranged with a selection of small and
large tiles for the most authentic look:
lay the tiles on the floor to plan the
setting out, then transfer them to the
wall one by one.

Irregularly-shaped stones can be
laid in any pattern you want, but again,
it's best to set them out on the floor to
achieve a good balance of large and
small sizes for realism.

With some stone tiles you have to
coat the wall with a special mortar-
coloured adhesive which gives an
overall background, then stick the
individual tiles on by buttering their
backs with adhesive.

FIXING POLYSTYRENE
CEILING TILES

Where to use the tiles
Polystyrene tiles can be used in
virtually any room in the house except
the kitchen, where they would be
directly over a source of heat.

Setting out the ceiling
Remove any friable material and make
sure the ceiling is clean and free from
grease. Snap two chalked lines which
cross each other at right angles in the
centre of the ceiling. Hang the tiles to
the chalked lines, checking their
alignment frequently.

Applying the tiles
Use a proprietary polystyrene adhesive
or a heavy-duty wallpaper paste.
Spread the adhesive across the back of
the tile to cover all but the very edge.

Press the first tile into one of the
angles formed by the marked lines. Use
the flat of your hand: fingertip pressure
can crush polystyrene. Proceed with
subsequent tiles to complete one half of
the ceiling, then the other.

Cutting the tiles
Mark the border tiles, then, on a flat
piece of board, cut through them with a
single stroke, using a sharp trimming
knife with a long blade. Clean up the
edges, but take care not to rub them too
hard or the polystyrene granules will
crumble away.

Mark out curves with a card
template, then follow the marked line
freehand with a trimming knife.

SETTING OUT

FOR SOFT

FLOOR TILES

SEE ALSO
Details for:
Floor tiles   60-61

SETTING OUT FOR DIAGONAL TILING

Arranging tiles diagonally can create an unusual decorative effect, especially if your choice of tiles enables you to mix colours. Setting out and laying the tiles off centre is not complicated – it's virtually the same as fixing them at right-angles, except that you will be working towards a corner instead of a straight wall. Mark a centre line, and bisect it at right-angles using an improvised compass (see right). Draw a line from opposite diagonal corners of the room through the centre point. Dry-lay a row of tiles to plot the margins (see below right). Mark a right angle to the diagonal. Fix a batten along one diagonal as a guide to laying the first row of tiles.

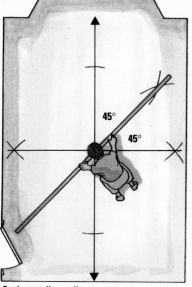

Setting out diagonally
Bisect the quartered room at 45 degrees.

Vinyl, rubber, cork and carpet tiles are relatively large, so you can complete the floor fairly quickly. Some vinyl tiles are self-adhesive, and carpet tiles are loose-laid, both of which speed up the process still further. Soft tiles such as these can be cut easily with a sharp trimming knife or even scissors, so fitting to irregular shapes is easier.

Marking out the floor

It is possible to lay soft tiles onto either a solid-concrete or suspended wooden floor, provided the surface is level, clean and dry. Most soft tiles can be set out in a similar way: find the centre of two opposite walls and snap a chalked string between them to mark a line across the floor (**1**). Lay loose tiles at right angles to the line up to one wall (see below left). If there is a gap of less than half a tile-width, move the line sideways by half a tile in order to give a wider margin.

To draw a line at right angles to the first, use string and a pencil as an improvised compass to scribe arcs on the marked line, at equal distances each side of the centre (**2**).

From each point, scribe arcs on both sides of the line (**3**), which bisect each other. Join the points to form a line across the room (**4**). As before, lay tiles at right angles to the new line to make sure border tiles are at least half-width. Nail a guide batten against one line to align the first row of tiles.

If the room is noticeably irregular in shape, centre the first line on the fireplace or the door opening (see below right).

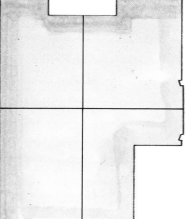

Setting out
A quartered room ensures that the tiles are laid symmetrically. This method is suitable for the following tiles: vinyl, rubber, cork and carpet.

4 Right angle complete

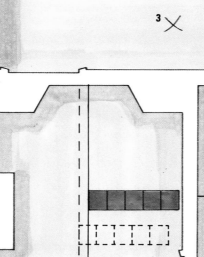

Plotting margin width (*near right*)
Lay loose tiles to make sure there is a reasonable gap at the margins. If not, move the line half a tile-width to the left.

Plotting an odd-shaped room (*far right*)
When a room is not a single rectangle, set out the lines using the fireplace and door as focal points.

LAYING VINYL
FLOOR TILES

Tiles precoated with adhesive can be laid quickly and simply, and there is no risk of squeezing glue onto the surface. If you are not using self-adhesive tiles, however, follow the tile-manufacturer's instructions concerning the type of adhesive to use.

Fixing self-adhesive tiles

Stack the tiles in the room for 24 hours before you lay them so they become properly acclimatized.

If the tiles have a directional pattern – some have arrows printed on the back to indicate this – make sure you lay them the correct way.

Remove the protective paper backing from the first tile prior to laying **(1)**, then press the edge against the guide batten. Align one corner with the centre line **(2)**. Gradually lower the tile onto the floor and press it down.

Lay the next tile on the other side of the line, butting against the first one **(3)**. Form a square with two more tiles. Lay tiles around the square to form a pyramid **(4)**. Continue in this way to fill one half of the room, remove the batten and tile the other half.

1 Peel paper backing from self-adhesive tiles

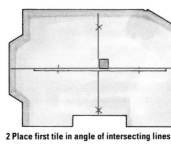

2 Place first tile in angle of intersecting lines

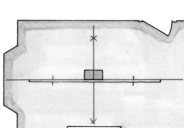

3 Butt up next tile on other side of line

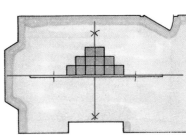

4 Lay tiles in a pyramid, then complete half room

GLUING VINYL TILES

Spread adhesive thinly but evenly across the floor, using a notched spreader and covering an area for two to three tiles only. Lay the tiles carefully and wipe adhesive from their faces.

Apply bed of adhesive with notched spreader

Single threshold bar

Finishing off the floor

As soon as you have laid all the floor tiles, wash over the surface with a damp cloth to remove any finger marks. It is not often necessary to polish vinyl tiles, but you can apply an emulsion floor polish if you wish.

Fit a straight metal strip (available from carpet suppliers) over the edge of the tiles when you finish at a doorway. When the tiles butt up to an area of carpet, fit a single threshold bar onto the edge of the carpeting (see left).

CUTTING TILES TO FIT

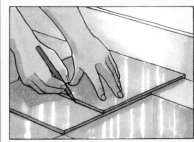

Trimming border tiles
Edges are rarely square, so cut border tiles to the skirting profile. To make a border tile, lay a loose one exactly on top of the last full tile. Place another tile on top, but with its edge touching the wall. Draw along the edge of this tile with a pencil to mark the tile below. Remove the marked tile and cut along the line, then fit the cut-off portion of the tile into the border.

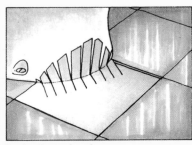

Cutting irregular shapes
To fit curves and mouldings, make a template for each tile out of thin card. Cut fingers which can be pressed against the object to reproduce its shape. Transfer the template to a tile and cut it out. You can also use a profile gauge to mark tiles when you are cutting complex curves.

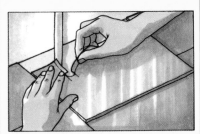

Fitting around pipes
Mark the position of the pipe on the tile using a compass. Draw parallel lines to the edge of the tile, taken from the perimeter of the circle. Measure halfway between the lines and cut a straight slit to the edge of the tile. Fold back the slit and slide the tile in place.

Carpet tiles

Carpet tiles are laid as for vinyl tiles, except that they are not usually glued down. Set out centre lines on the floor, but don't fit a guide batten: simply aligning the row of tiles with the marked lines is sufficient.

Carpet tiles have a pile which must be laid in the correct direction. This is sometimes indicated by arrows marked on the back of each tile.

Some tiles have ridges of rubber on the back which mean they will slip easily in one direction, but not in another. The non-slip direction is typically denoted by an arrow on the back of the tile. It is usual to lay the tiles in pairs so that one prevents the other from moving. In any case, stick down every third row of tiles using double-sided carpet tape, and tape squares in those areas where there is likely to be heavy traffic.

Cut and fit carpet tiles as described for vinyl tiles.

Checking direction of pile
Some carpet tiles have arrows on the back to indicate the direction in which they should be laid.

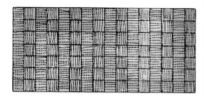

Using pile for decoration
Two typical arrangements of tiles, using the pile to make decorative textures.

Cork tiles

Use the methods described for laying vinyl tiles to cut and fit cork tiles, but use a contact adhesive: thixotropic types allow a degree of movement as you position the tiles.

Make sure the tiles are level by tapping down the edges with a block of wood. Unfinished tiles can be sanded lightly to remove minor irregularities.

Vacuum then seal unfinished tiles with two to three coats of clear varnish.

Bedding cork tiles
Bed the edges of cork tiles with a woodblock.

Rubber tiles

Use the same methods for laying rubber tiles as for vinyl types. Use a latex flooring adhesive.

Laying rubber tiles
Lay large rubber tiles by placing one edge and corner against neighbouring tiles before lowering onto a bed of adhesive.

NEAT DETAILING FOR SOFT FLOOR TILES

Covering a plinth
Create the impression of a floating bath panel or kitchen base units by running floor tiles up the face of the plinth. Hold carpet tiles into a tight bend with gripper strip (1) or glue other tiles in place for a similar detail. Glue a plastic moulding, normally used to seal around the edge of a bath, behind the floor covering to produce a curved detail which makes cleaning the floor a lot easier (2).

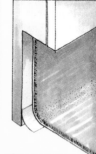

1 Sharp bend with gripper strip **2 Curved detail for easy cleaning**

Cutting holes for pipes
With most soft floor tiles you can cut neat holes for central-heating pipes using a home-made punch: cut a 150mm (6in) length of the same diameter pipe and sharpen the rim on the inside at one end with a metalworking file. Plot the position for the hole on the tile, then place the punching tool on top. Hit the other end of the punch with a hammer to cut through the tile cleanly. With some carpet tiles you may have to cut round the backing to release the cut-out and prevent fraying with tape.

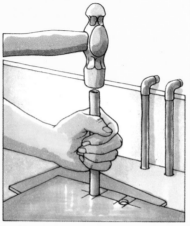

Punch holes for pipes with sharpened offcut

SEE ALSO

● **Access to plumbing**
If you are covering a bath panel with tiles, remember to make a lift-off section in the panel to gain access to pipes and tap fittings beneath the bath tub.

LAYING CERAMIC FLOOR TILES

● **Battens on concrete**
Use masonry nails to hold battens onto a concrete floor.

Ceramic floor tiles make a durable, hard surface that can also be extremely decorative. Laying the tiles on a floor is similar to hanging them on a wall, except that because floor tiles are somewhat thicker than wall tiles you have to be especially careful when cutting them to fit in order to achieve neat and accurate results.

Setting out

To lay ceramic tiles on a suspended wooden floor, cover it first with 12mm (½in) plywood to make a solid, level surface that will not flex. A flat, dry concrete floor is an ideal base in itself.

Mark out the floor as for soft floor tiles and work out the spacing to achieve even, fairly wide border tiles. Nail two softwood guide battens to the floor, set at a right angle and aligned with the last row of whole tiles on two adjacent walls farthest from the door. Even a small error will become obvious by the time you reach the other end of the room, so check the angle by measuring three units from one corner along one batten and four units along the other. Measure the diagonal between the marks: it should measure five units if the battens form an angle of 90 degrees. Make a final check by dry-laying a square of tiles in the angle.

Laying the tiles

Use a proprietary floor-tile adhesive that is waterproof and slightly flexible when set. Spread it on with a plain or notched trowel, according to the manufacturer's recommendations. The normal procedure is to apply adhesive to the floor for the main area of tiling and to butter the backs of cut tiles.

Spread enough adhesive on the floor for about 16 tiles. Press the tiles into the adhesive, starting in the corner. Work along both battens, then fill in between to form the square. Few floor tiles have spacing lugs, so use plastic spacers.

● **Grouting the joints**
Grout the tiles as for walls, but fill the joints almost flush rather than indenting them. A dark grout is less likely to look dirty after a time.

Check the alignment of the tiles with a straightedge and make sure that they are lying flat by checking them with a spirit level. Work your way along one batten, laying squares of 16 tiles each time. Tile the rest of the floor in the same way, working back towards the door. Leave the adhesive to dry for 24 hours before you walk on the floor to remove the guide battens and fit the border tiles.

Cutting ceramic floor tiles

Measure and cut the tiles to fit the border as described for wall tiles. Because they are thicker, floor tiles will not snap quite so easily, so if you have a large area to fill, use a tile-cutting jig.

Alternatively, make your own device by nailing two scraps of 12mm (½in) thick plywood to 50 x 25mm (2 x 1in) softwood battens, leaving a parallel gap between them which is just wide enough to take a tile. Hold the device on edge, insert a scored tile into the gap, up to the scored line – which should be uppermost – and press down on the free end (see below right). Snap thin strips from the edge in this way. Saw or nibble curved shapes.

Setting out for tiling
Mark out the floor as for soft floor tiles, then set out the field with battens.
1 Fix temporary guide battens at the edge of the field on the two adjacent walls farthest from the door.
2 Ensure that the battens are at true right angles by measuring the diagonal.
3 Dry-lay a square of 16 tiles in the angles as a final check.

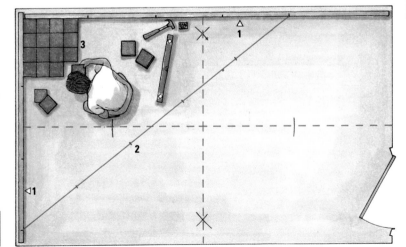

LAYING MOSAIC FLOOR TILES

Set out mosaic floor tiles as for ceramic floor tiles. Spread on the adhesive, then lay the tiles, paper-facing uppermost, with spacers that match the gaps between individual pieces. Press the sheets into the adhesive, using a block of wood to tamp them level. Twenty-four hours later, remove the spacers and soak off the facing with warm water. Grout as normal.

If you have to fit a sheet of mosaic tiles around an obstruction, remove individual mosaic pieces as close to the profile as possible. Fit the sheet (**1**), then cut and replace the pieces to fit around the shapes.

If you are using mosaics in areas of hard wear, such as patio steps, protect vulnerable edges with a nosing of ordinary ceramic floor tiles to match or contrast with the main field of tiles (**2**).

1 Remove mosaic pieces to fit around pipe

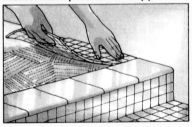

2 Lay a nosing of ceramic tiles on step treads

Using a home-made jig
It is essential to ensure that the marked line is positioned parallel to the edge of the plywood or the tile will not snap accurately. Protect your eyes with goggles.

LAYING QUARRY TILES

Quarry tiles, being tough and hardwearing, are the best choice for floors that will receive heavy use. However, they are relatively thick and making even a straight cut is not easy. Reserve them for areas that don't require a lot of complex shaping.

Don't lay quarry tiles on a suspended wooden floor; replace the floorboards with 18 or 22mm (¾ or 1in) exterior-grade plywood to provide a sufficiently flat and rigid base. A concrete floor presents no problems, as long as it is free from damp. Provided the floor is reasonably flat, the mortar bed on which the tiles are laid will take care of fine levelling.

Setting out for tiling

Set out two guide battens in a corner of the room at right angles to each other, as described for ceramic floor tiles, opposite. The depth of the battens should measure about twice the thickness of the tiles to allow for the mortar bed. Fix them temporarily to a concrete floor with long masonry nails. The level of the battens is essential, so check with a spirit level; pack out under the battens with scraps of hardboard or card where necessary. Mark tile widths along each batten, leaving 3mm (⅛in) gaps between for grouting, as a guide to positioning.

Dry-lay a square of 16 tiles in the angle, then nail a third batten to the floor, butting against the tiles and parallel with one of the other battens. Level and mark it as before.

Bedding down the tiles

Lay quarry tiles on a bed of mortar made from 1 part cement : 3 parts builder's sand. When water is added, the mortar should be stiff enough to hold an impression when squeezed.

Soak quarry tiles in water prior to laying to prevent them absorbing water from the mortar too rapidly, causing poor adhesion. Cut a stout board to span the parallel battens: this will be used to level the mortar bed and tiles. Cut a notch in each end to fit between the battens (see right). In depth, each notch should match the thickness of a tile less 3mm (⅛in).

Spread the mortar to a depth of about 12mm (½in) to cover the area of 16 tiles. Level the mortar by dragging the notched side of the board across it.

Dust dry cement on the mortar, then lay the tiles along three sides of the square against the battens. Fill in the square, spacing the tiles by adjusting them with a trowel. Tamp down the tiles gently with the un-notched side of the board until they are level with the battens. If the mortar is too stiff, brush water into the joints. Wipe mortar from the faces of the tiles before it hardens.

Fill in between the battens, then move one batten back to form another bay of the same size. Level it to match the first section. Tile section-by-section until the main floor is complete. When the floor is hard enough to walk on, lift the battens and fill in with border tiles.

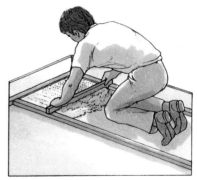

Setting out a quarry-tiled floor
The method for laying quarry tiles is similar to the one used for glazed ceramic tiles.
1 Fix two guide battens – about twice the tile thickness – at right angles to each other.
2 Fix a third batten parallel with one of the others.
3 Dry-lay 16 tiles between the battens to check their accuracy, then proceed with tiling.

CUTTING QUARRY TILES

Quarry tiles are so thick that the only practicable method for cutting them is to use a robust jig. Choose one that is designed to cut tiles up to 18mm (¾in) thick. It should also incorporate a tungsten-carbide cutting wheel and an adjustable fence to facilitate fast and accurate work.

Having scored the cut line once only, locate the tile in the jaws of the tool and press down on the long lever arm to snap the tile cleanly.

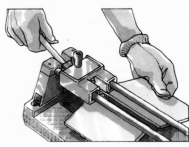

Snap thick quarry tiles with a tile-cutting jig

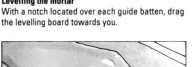

Levelling the mortar
With a notch located over each guide batten, drag the levelling board towards you.

Notching the levelling board
Cut matching notches at each end of the board for levelling the mortar.

Levelling border tiles
Use a notched piece of plywood to level the mortar and tamp down the tiles with a block.

● **Finishing off the quarry tiling**
Grout quarry tiles as for ceramic floor tiles, using cement or proprietary waterproof grout. Clean it off the surface by sprinkling sawdust onto it and wiping off with a cloth. Wash the finished floor with a soapless detergent.

LAYING
SHEET VINYL

Sheet vinyl is ideal wall-to-wall floorcovering for kitchens, utility rooms and bathrooms, where you are bound to spill water from time to time. There are numerous colours, patterns and embossed effects available, and you will find most types straightforward to lay if you follow a systematic routine.

Leave the vinyl in a room for 24 to 48 hours before laying, preferably opened flat or at least stood on end, loosely rolled. Assuming there are no seams, start by fitting against the longest wall first. Drive a nail through a wooden lath about 50mm (2in) from one end.

Pull the vinyl away from the wall by approximately 35mm (1½in). Make sure it is parallel with the wall or the main axis of the room. Use the nailed strip to scribe a line following the skirting (**1**). Cut the vinyl with a knife or scissors and slide the sheet up against the wall.

To get the rest of the sheet to lie as flat as possible, cut a triangular notch at each corner. Make a straight cut down to the floor at external corners. Remove as much waste as possible, leaving 50 to 75mm (2 to 3in) turned up all round.

Press the vinyl into the angle between skirting and floor with a bolster. Align a metal straightedge with the crease and run along it with a sharp knife held at a slight angle to the skirting (**2**). If your trimming is less than perfect, nail a cover strip of quadrant moulding to the skirting.

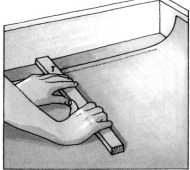
1 Fit to first wall by scribing with a nailed strip

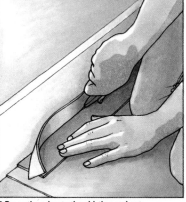

Trimming and gluing vinyl sheet

Trimming to fit a doorway
Work around the doorframe moulding making straight cuts and removing triangular notches at each change of angle as if they were miniature corners. Crease the vinyl against the floor and trim the waste. Make a straight cut across the opening and fit a threshold bar over the edge of the sheet.

Cutting around an obstruction
To fit around a WC pan or basin pedestal, fold back the sheet and pierce it with a knife just above floor level. Draw a blade up towards the edge. Make triangular cuts around the base, gradually working around the curve until the sheet can lie flat on the floor (**3**). Crease and cut off the waste.

Sticking the sheet
Modern vinyls can be loose-laid but you may prefer to glue the edges, especially along a door opening. Peel back the edge and spread a band of the recommended flooring adhesive with a toothed spreader (**4**) or use a 50mm (2in) wide double-sided adhesive tape.

Making a join
If you have to join widths of vinyl, scribe one edge as described above, then overlap the free edge with the second sheet until the pattern matches exactly. Cut through both pieces with a knife, then remove the waste strips.

Without moving the sheets, fold back both cut edges, apply tape or adhesive and press the join together.

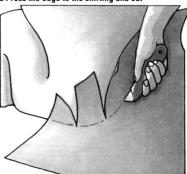
2 Press the edge to the skirting and cut

3 Make triangular cuts around a curve

Positioning the vinyl
Aligning the vinyl sheet squarely on the floor is essential.
1 Fit to the longest, uninterrupted wall.
2 Cut triangular notches at each external and internal corner so the sheet will lie flat.
3 Allow folds of about 75mm (3in) all round for scribing to fit accurately.
4 Make a straight cut against the door opening so a threshold bar can be fixed.

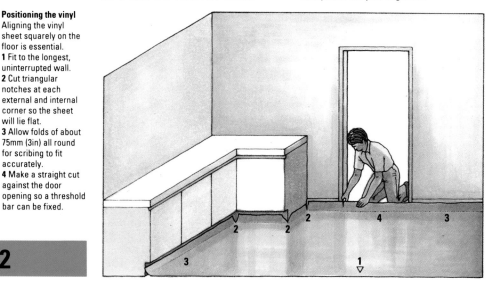

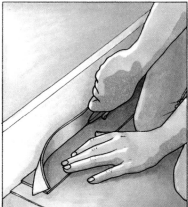
4 Secure butting edges on a bed of adhesive

DECORATING
TOOLS

DECORATOR'S TOOL KIT

Most home owners collect a fairly extensive kit of tools for decorating their houses or flats. Although traditionalists will want to stick to tried-and-tested tools and to materials of proven reliability, others may prefer to try recent innovations aimed at making the work easier and faster for the home decorator.

TOOLS FOR PREPARATION

Whether you are tiling, painting or papering, make sure the surface to which the materials will be applied is sound and clean.

Straight scraper

Serrated scraper

Wallpaper and paint scrapers
The wide stiff blade of a scraper is for removing softened paint or soaked paper. The best scrapers have high-quality steel blades and riveted rosewood handles. One with a blade 100 to 125mm (4 to 5in) wide is best for stripping wallpaper, while a narrow one, no more than 25mm (1in) wide, is better for removing paint from window frames and doorframes.

A serrated scraper will score impervious wallcoverings so that water or stripping solution can penetrate faster – but take care not to damage the wall itself.

Vinyl gloves
Most people wear ordinary household 'rubber' gloves as protection for their hands when washing down or preparing paintwork – but tough PVC work gloves are more hard-wearing and will protect your skin against many harmful chemicals.

WOODWORKING TOOLS

As well as the decorating tools described here, you will need a basic woodworking tool kit for repairing damaged floorboards or window frames and for jobs such as installing wall panelling or laying parquet flooring.

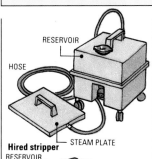

RESERVOIR

HOSE

STEAM PLATE

Hired stripper
RESERVOIR

STEAM PLATE

Lightweight stripper

Steam wallpaper stripper
To remove wallpaper quickly (especially thick wallcoverings), either buy or hire an electric steam-generating stripper.

All steam strippers work on similar principles – but follow any specific safety instructions that come with the machine.

Using a steam stripper
Fill the stripper's reservoir with water and plug the tool into a socket outlet. Hold the steaming plate against the wallpaper until it is soft enough to be removed with a scraper. You will find that some wallcoverings take longer to soften than others.

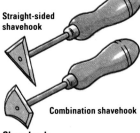

Straight-sided shavehook

Combination shavehook

Shavehook
This is a special scraper for removing old paint and varnish. A straight-sided triangular shavehook is fine for flat surfaces, but one with a combination blade can be used on concave and convex mouldings too. You pull a shavehook towards you to remove the softened paint.

Hot-air stripper
The gas blowtorch was once the professional's tool for softening old paint that required stripping, but the modern electric hot-air stripper is much easier to use. It is as efficient as a blowtorch, but there's less risk of scorching woodwork. With most strippers, you can adjust the temperature. The interchangeable nozzles are shaped to concentrate the heated air or direct it away from window panes.

Filling knife
A filling knife looks like a paint scraper, but has a flexible blade for forcing filler into cracks in timber or plaster. Large areas of damaged wall should be patched with a plasterer's trowel.

Handbrush

Cup brushes

Wire brushes
You can use a handbrush with steel-wire 'bristles' to remove flaking paint and particles of rust from metalwork before repainting it. However, the job is easier if you use a rotary wire cup brush fitted into the chuck of an electric drill, wearing goggles or safety glasses to protect your eyes.

Mastic guns
Non-setting mastic, which is permanently flexible, is used to seal joints between materials with different rates of expansion that would eventually crack and eject a rigid filler. You can buy mastic that you squeeze direct from a plastic tube, but it's more easily applied from a cartridge clipped into a spring-loaded gun.

Tack rag
A resin-impregnated cloth called a 'tack rag' is ideal for picking up particles of dust and hard paint from a surface that's been prepared for painting. If you can't get a tack rag, use a lint-free cloth dampened with white spirit.

Dusting brush
A dusting brush has long soft bristles for clearing dust out of mouldings and crevices just before painting. You can use an ordinary paintbrush, provided that you keep it clean and dry.

WET-AND-DRY PAPER

Wet-and-dry abrasive paper is used for smoothing new paint-work or varnish before applying the final coat. It consists of silicon-carbide particles glued to a waterproof backing paper. Dip a piece in water and rub the paintwork until a slurry of paint and water forms. Wipe it off with a cloth before it dries; then rinse the paper clean and continue.

● **Essential tools**
Wallpaper scraper
Combination shavehook
Filling knife
Hot-air stripper
Wire brush

73

DECORATING TOOLS

Paint kettle
To carry paint to a work site, decant a little into a cheap, lightweight plastic paint kettle.

● **Essential tools**
Flat brushes 12, 25 and 50mm (½, 1 and 2in)
Wall brush 150mm (6in)

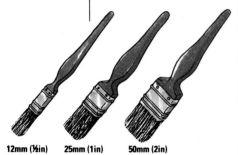

12mm (½in)   25mm (1in)   50mm (2in)

Flat paintbrush
The filling is set in rubber – or pitch or resin – and bound to the wooden or plastic handle with a pressed-metal ferrule. You will need several sizes, up to 50mm (2in), for painting, varnishing and staining woodwork.

PAINTBRUSHES

Some paintbrushes are made from natural animal hair. Hog bristle is the best, but it is often mixed with inferior horsehair or oxhair to reduce cost.

Synthetic-bristle brushes are generally the least expensive, and are quite adequate for the home decorator.

Bristle types
Bristle is ideal for paintbrushes since each hair tapers naturally and splits at the tip into even finer filaments that hold paint well. Bristle is also tough and resilient. Synthetic 'bristle' (usually made of nylon) is designed to resemble the characteristics of real bristle, and a good-quality nylon brush will serve most painters as well as a bristle one.

Choosing a brush
The bristles of a good brush – the 'filling' – are densely packed. When you fan them with your fingers they should spring back into shape immediately. Flex the tip of the brush against your hand to see if any bristles work loose. Even a good brush will shed a few bristles at first, but never clumps. The ferrule should be fixed firmly to the handle.

One-knot paintbrush
The bristles of a one-knot paintbrush are bound to a cylindrical handle with string or wire or a metal ferrule.

The grouping of the bristles makes them very resilient – but when flexed against a surface, they will fan out like those of the commoner flat paintbrush.

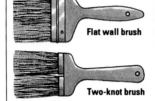

Flat wall brush

Two-knot brush

Wall brush
To apply emulsion paint by brush, use a 150mm (6in) flat wall brush or a two-knot brush of the kind favoured by continental painters and decorators.

Cutting-in brush
The filling of a cutting-in brush, or 'bevelled sash tool', is cut at an angle so that you can paint moulded glazing bars right up into the corners and against the glass. Most painters make do with a 12mm (½in) flat brush.

STENCIL AND GRAIN-EFFECT TOOLS

Stencil brush
A stencil brush has short stiff bristles. The paint is stippled through or around a cut-out template that defines the shape to be painted.

Grainers
You can buy special brushes for creating wood-grain effects with paint or varnish. A 'mottler' has a dense soft filling of squirrel hair for lifting bands or streaks of colour to simulate figured hardwoods. A 'pencil grainer' has a row of fine brushes mounted in one handle for drawing patterns of parallel lines.

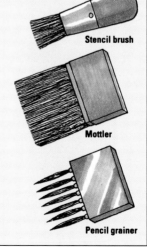

Stencil brush

Mottler

Pencil grainer

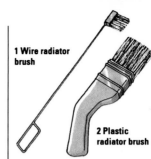

1 Wire radiator brush

2 Plastic radiator brush

Radiator brush
Unless you take a radiator off the wall for decorating, you will need a special brush to paint the back of it and the wall behind it. There are two types of radiator brush: the one has a standard flat paintbrush head at right angles to a long wire handle (**1**); the other is like an ordinary paintbrush but has an angled plastic handle (**2**).

Banister brush
A household banister brush gives excellent results when used for painting rough or rendered walls.

Paint shield

Glass scraper

Paint shield and scraper
There are various plastic and metal shields for protecting glass when you are painting window frames and glazing bars. If the glass does get spattered, it can be cleaned with a blade clipped into a special holder.

CLEANING PAINTBRUSHES

● **Water-based paints**
As soon as you finish working, wash the bristles with warm soapy water, flexing them between your fingers to work the paint out of the roots. Then rinse the brush in clean water and shake out the excess. Smooth the bristles and slip an elastic band round their tips to hold the shape of the filling while it is drying.

Holding the shape of a brush

● **Solvent-based paints**
If you are using solvent-based paints, you can suspend the brush overnight in enough water to cover the bristles, then blot it with kitchen paper before you resume painting.

When you have finished painting, brush out excess paint onto newspaper, then flex the bristles in a bowl of thinners. Some finishes need special thinners – so check for this on the container. Otherwise, use white spirit or a chemical brush cleaner. Wash the dirty thinners from the bristles with hot soapy water, then rinse the brush.

Soaking a brush

● **Hardened paint**
If paint has hardened on a brush, soften it by soaking the bristles in brush cleaner. It will then become water-soluble and will wash out easily with hot water. If the old paint is very stubborn, dip the bristles in some paint stripper.

STORING PAINTBRUSHES

Before storing, fold soft paper over the filling and secure it to the ferrule with an elastic band.

DECORATING
TOOLS

PAINT PADS

Paint pads help inexperienced decorators to apply paints and wood dyes quickly and evenly. They are not universally popular, but no one would dispute their usefulness for painting large flat areas. Paint pads should not drip paint provided that they are loaded properly.

Standard pads
There is a range of rectangular paint pads for decorating walls, ceilings and flat woodwork. These standard pads have short mohair pile on their painting surfaces and are generally made with D-shape handles.

Edging pad
An easy way to paint a straight edge – between a wall and a ceiling, for example – is to use an edging pad with small wheels or rollers that guide it parallel to the adjacent surface.

Sash pad
A sash pad has a small mohair sole for painting the glazing bars of sash windows. Most sash pads incorporate plastic guides to stop them straying onto the glass.

POWER ROLLER

With a power roller you can paint continuously for as long as the batteries last – about five hours. Paint is delivered from the portable reservoir, via a flexible hose, to the roller head. Because you don't have to keep reloading the roller, you can work very quickly, covering about 1sq m (1sq yd) per minute. To wash the roller, connect its hose to a tap and flush water through the roller head.

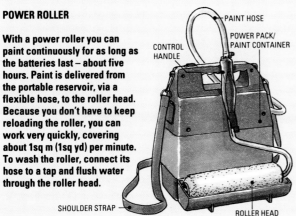

PAINT HOSE
POWER PACK/PAINT CONTAINER
CONTROL HANDLE
SHOULDER STRAP
ROLLER HEAD

CLEANING PAINT PADS

Before dipping a new pad into paint for the first time, brush it with a clothes brush to remove any loose nylon filaments.

● When you finish painting, blot the pad on old newspaper, then wash it in the appropriate solvent – water, white spirit or brush cleaner, or any special thinners recommended by the paint manufacturer. Squeeze the foam and rub the pile with gloved fingertips, then wash the pad in hot soapy water and rinse it.

● A new paint pad that has just been used for the first time may appear to be stained by paint even after it has been washed. However, the colour will not contaminate the next batch of fresh paint.

Pad tray
Pads and trays are normally sold as sets; but if you buy a separate tray, get one with a loading roller that distributes paint evenly onto the sole of a pad drawn across it.

PAINT ROLLERS

A paint roller is the ideal tool for painting a large area of wall or ceiling quickly. The cylindrical sleeves that actually apply the paint are interchangeable, and slide onto a revolving sprung-wire cage fitted to the cranked handle of the roller. The sleeves are very easy to swap or remove for washing.

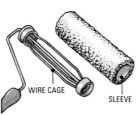

WIRE CAGE
SLEEVE

Sizes of roller sleeves
Sleeves for standard paint rollers are 175mm (7in) or 225mm (9in) long, but it is also possible to buy 300mm (1ft) rollers.

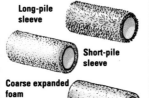

Long-pile sleeve
Short-pile sleeve
Coarse expanded foam
Moulded PVC

Types of roller sleeves
You can buy roller sleeves of various materials to suit different surface textures and kinds of paint. Most sleeves are made of *sheepskin* or *synthetic fibres* cropped to different lengths. A sheepskin sleeve can hold more paint than one that is made from synthetic fibre, but costs about 25 per cent more.

Choose a *long-pile sleeve* for emulsion or masonry paint on rough or textured surfaces. A *medium-pile sleeve* is best for emulsion or satin-finish oil paints on smooth surfaces. It is also ideal for applying solid emulsion. For gloss paints, use a *short-pile sleeve*.

Cheap *plastic-foam sleeves* are unsatisfactory both for oil paints and emulsions. They leave tiny air bubbles in the painted surface, and the foam often distorts as it dries after washing. But they are cheap enough to be thrown away after use with finishes such as bituminous paint that would be difficult to remove even from a short-pile sleeve.

Use a *coarse expanded-foam sleeve* for applying textured paints and coatings. There are also *moulded PVC rollers* with embossed surfaces to pattern high-build textured coatings.

Extending a pad or roller
If your paint pad or roller has a hollow handle, you can plug it onto a telescopic extension handle to enable you to reach a ceiling from the floor.

CLEANING A ROLLER

Remove most of the excess paint by running the roller backwards and forwards across some old newspaper. If you are planning to use the roller next day, apply a few drops of the appropriate thinners to the sleeve and then wrap it in plastic. Otherwise, clean, wash and rinse the sleeve before the paint has time to dry.

● **Water-based paints**
If you've been using emulsion or acrylic paint, flush most of it out under running water, then massage a little liquid detergent into the pile of the sleeve and flush it again.

● **Solvent-based paints**
To remove solvent-based paints, pour some thinners into the roller tray and slowly roll the sleeve back and forth in it. Squeeze the roller and agitate the pile with gloved hands. When the paint has dissolved, wash the sleeve in hot soapy water.

Roller tray
A paint roller is loaded from a sloping plastic or metal tray, the deep end of which acts as a paint reservoir. Load the roller by rolling paint from the deep end up and down the tray's ribbed slope once or twice, so as to get even distribution on the sleeve.

1   2   3

1 Corner roller
You cannot paint into a corner with a standard roller, so unless there are to be different adjacent colours, paint the corner first with a shaped corner roller.
2 Pipe roller
A pipe roller has two narrow sleeves, mounted side by side, which locate over the cylindrical pipework to paint it.
3 Radiator roller
This is a thin roller on a long wire handle for painting behind radiators and pipes.

● **Essential tools**
50 and 200mm (2 and 8in) standard pads
Sash pad
Large roller and selection of sleeves
Roller tray

DECORATING TOOLS

PAINTSPRAYING EQUIPMENT

Spraying is so fast and efficient that it's worth considering if you plan to paint the outside walls of a building. The equipment is expensive to buy, but it can be rented from tool-hire outlets. You can spray most exterior paints and finishes if they are thinned properly, but tell the hire company which paint you intend to use, so they can supply the right spray gun with the correct nozzle. Acquire goggles and a respirator at the same time.

Preparation
As far as possible, plan to work on a dry and windless day. Also, allow time to mask off windows, doors and pipework.

Follow the setting-up and handling instructions supplied with the equipment; and if you are new to the work, practise beforehand on an inconspicuous section of wall.

Compressor-operated spray
With this equipment, the paint is mixed with compressed air to emerge as a fine spray. Some compressors deliver air to an intermediate tank and top it up as the air is drawn off by the spray gun, but most hired compressors supply air directly to the gun.

The trigger opens a valve to admit air, and at the same time opens the paint outlet at the nozzle. The paint is drawn from a container, usually mounted below the gun, and mixes with air at the tip. Most guns have air-delivery horns at the sides of the nozzle to produce a fan-shaped spray.

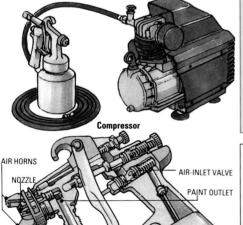

Spraying reinforced paints
Hire a special gravity-fed spray gun to apply reinforced masonry paint and 'Tyrolean' finishes. The material is loaded into a hopper on top of the gun.

Compressor

AIR HORNS
NOZZLE
AIR-INLET VALVE
PAINT OUTLET
TRIGGER

Spray gun

Airless sprayer
In an airless sprayer, an electric pump delivers the paint itself at high pressure to the spray gun. The paint is picked up through a plastic tube inserted in the paint container, and the pump forces it through a high-pressure hose to a filter and pressure regulator, which is adjustable to produce the required spray pattern.

The paint leaves the nozzle at such high pressure that it can penetrate skin. Most spray guns of this kind therefore have safety shields on their nozzles.

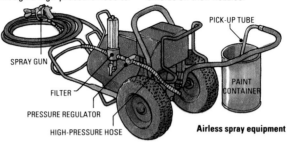

SPRAY GUN
FILTER
PRESSURE REGULATOR
HIGH-PRESSURE HOSE
PICK-UP TUBE
PAINT CONTAINER

Airless spray equipment

USING SPRAYERS SAFELY

Follow safety recommendations supplied with the sprayer, and take the following precautions:

● Wear goggles and a respirator when spraying.
● Don't spray indoors without proper extraction equipment.
● Atomized oil paint is highly flammable, so extinguish any naked lights and never smoke when you are spraying.
● Never leave the equipment unattended, especially where there are children or pets.
● If the gun has a safety lock, always engage it whenever you are not actually spraying.
● Unplug the equipment and release the pressure in the hose before trying to clear a blocked nozzle.
● Never aim the gun at yourself or anyone else. If you should accidentally spray your skin at close quarters with an airless gun, then seek medical advice immediately.

CLEANING A SPRAY GUN

Empty out any paint that is left in the container and add some thinners. Spray the thinners until they emerge clear, then release the pressure and dismantle the spray nozzle. Clean the parts with a solvent-dampened rag and wipe out the container.

COMMON SPRAYING FAULTS

Streaked paintwork
An uneven, streaked finish will result if you do not overlap the passes of the gun.

Patchy paintwork
Coverage won't be consistent if you move the gun in an arc. Keep it pointing directly at the wall and moving parallel to it.

Orange-peel texture
A wrinkled paint film resembling the texture of orange peel is usually caused by spraying paint that is too thick. Alternatively, if the paint seems to be of the right consistency, you may be moving the gun too slowly.

Runs
Runs will occur if you apply too much paint – probably through holding the gun too close to the surface you are spraying.

Powdery finish
This is caused by paint drying before it reaches the wall. The remedy is to hold the gun a little closer to the wall's surface.

Spattering
If the pressure is too high, the finish will look speckled. To avoid spattering, lower the pressure till the finish is satisfactory.

Spitting
A partly clogged nozzle will make the gun splutter. Clear the nozzle with a stiff bristle from a brush – never use wire – and then wipe it with a rag dampened in thinners.

PAPERHANGER'S TOOLS

You can improvise some of the tools needed for paperhanging. However, even purpose-made equipment is inexpensive, so it's worth having a decent kit.

Tape measure
A retractable steel tape is best for measuring walls and ceilings in order to estimate the amount of wallcovering you will need.

Plumb bob and line

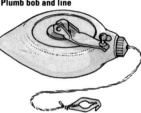

Retractable plumb line

Plumb line
Any small weight suspended on fine string can be used to mark the position of one edge of a strip of wallpaper. Hold the end of the line close to the ceiling, allow the weight to come to rest, and then mark the wall at points down the length of the line.

A purpose-made plumb line has a pointed metal weight called a plumb bob. The more-expensive versions have a string that retracts into a hollow plumb bob containing coloured chalk, so the string is coated with chalk every time it is withdrawn. With the string stretched taut, snap it like a bowstring to leave a chalk line on the wall.

Paste brush
Use either a wide wall brush or a short-pile roller to apply paste to the back of wallcoverings.

Clean either tool by washing it in warm water.

DECORATING
TOOLS

PASTING TABLE

You can paste wallcoverings on any flat surface, but a purpose-made pasting table provides a much more convenient working surface. It stands higher than the average dining table, but is only 25mm (1in) wider than a standard roll of wallpaper – which makes it easier to spread paste without getting it onto the worktop. The underframe folds flat and the top is hinged, enabling the table to be carried from room to room and stowed in a small space.

Paperhanger's brush
This is used for smoothing wall-coverings onto a wall or ceiling. Its bristles should be soft, so as not to damage delicate paper, but springy enough to provide the pressure to squeeze out air bubbles and excess paste. Wash the brush in warm water when you finish work to prevent paste hardening on the bristles.

Seam roller
Use a hardwood or plastic seam roller to press down the seams between strips of wallpaper – but don't use one on embossed or delicate wallcoverings.

Rubber   Felt

Smoothing roller
There are rubber rollers for squeezing trapped air from under wallcoverings, but use a felt one on delicate or flocked papers.

Paperhanger's scissors
Any fairly large scissors can be used for trimming wallpaper to length, but special paperhanger's scissors have extra-long blades to achieve a straight cut.

Craft knife
Use a knife to trim paper round light fittings and switches, and to achieve perfect butt joints by cutting through overlapping edges of paper. The knife must be extremely sharp to avoid tearing the paper, so use one with disposable blades that you can change as soon as one gets blunt. Some craft knives have short double-ended blades clamped in a metal or plastic handle. Others have long retractable blades that are snapped off in short sections to leave a new sharp point.

TILING TOOLS

Most of the tools in a tiler's kit are for applying ceramic wall and floor tiles, but others are used for laying soft tiles and vinyl sheeting.

Spirit level
You will need a spirit level for setting up temporary battens to align a field of tiles both horizontally and vertically.

Profile gauge
A profile gauge is used for copy-ing the shape of door mouldings or pipework to provide a pattern so you can fit soft floorcoverings.

As you press the steel pins of the gauge against the object you wish to copy, they slide back, replicating the shape. When you want to copy another shape, you press the needles against a flat surface to reposition them in a straight line.

Serrated trowel
Make a ridged bed for ceramic tiles by drawing the toothed edge of a plastic or steel tiler's trowel through the adhesive.

Tile cutter
A tile cutter has either a pointed tungsten-carbide tip or a steel wheel – like a glass cutter's – for scoring the glazed surface of ceramic tiles. The tile snaps cleanly along the scored line.

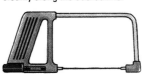

Tile saw
A tile saw has a bent-metal frame that holds a thin wire rod under tension. The rod is coated with particles of tungsten-carbide, which are hard enough to cut through ceramic tiles. As the rod is circular in section, it will cut in any direction, making it possible to saw straight and curved lines with equal ease.

Grout spreader
This tool has a hard-rubber blade mounted in a plastic handle. It is used for spreading grout into the gaps between ceramic tiles.

Nibblers
It is impossible to snap a very narrow strip off a ceramic tile. Instead score the line with a tile cutter, then break off the waste little by little with tile nibblers. They resemble pincers, but have sharper jaws of tungsten-carbide that open automatically when you relax your grip on the spring-loaded handles.

TILE-CUTTING JIGS

A jig makes it much easier to cut and fit tiles for the border around a field of tiles. With the one tool, you can measure the gap and cut the tiles to infill the border.

Using the jig
To measure the size of a border tile, slide the jig open until one pointer is against the adjacent wall and the other is against the edge of the last full tile (1). The jig automatically makes an allowance for grouting.

Fit the jig over the tile to be cut and use a tile cutter to score the glaze through the slot in the jig (2). The cutter comes with a pair of pliers with angled jaws for snapping the tile in two. Centre the scored line in the pliers' jaws, and squeeze the handles until the tile breaks cleanly (3).

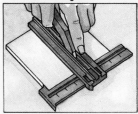

1 Measure the margin

2 Score the glazed surface

3 Snap the tile with special pliers

Floor-tile jig
Hire or buy a sturdy jig for marking and cutting quarry tiles and ceramic floor tiles.

● **Essential tools**
Steel tape measure
Plumb line
Paste brush
Paperhanger's brush
Seam roller
Scissors
Craft knife
Pasting table
Spirit level
Serrated trowel
Tile cutter and jig
Nibblers
Tile saw
Squeegee

GLOSSARY
OF TERMS

Aggregate
Powdered mica or particles of sand added to paint to create a textured finish.

Architrave
The moulding around a door or window.

Arris
The sharp edge at the meeting of two surfaces.

Baluster
One of a set of posts supporting a stair handrail.

Balustrade
The protective barrier alongside a staircase or landing.

Banister
See balustrade and baluster.

Batten
A narrow strip of wood.

Blind
To cover with sand.

Blown
To have broken away, as when a layer of cement rendering has parted from a wall.

Consumer unit
A box containing the house electrical-circuit fuses or miniature circuit breakers. A consumer unit is fitted with a master switch that turns off the supply of electricity to the whole building.

Cornice
The continuous horizontal moulding between the walls and ceiling.

Coving
A prefabricated moulding used to make a cornice.

Dado
The lower part of an interior wall – usually defined with a moulded rail.

Drop
A strip of wallpaper cut roughly to length ready for pasting to a wall.

Efflorescence
A white powdery deposit caused by soluble salts migrating to the surface of a wall or ceiling.

End grain
The surface of wood exposed after cutting across the fibres.

Fascia board
The strip of wood that covers the ends of rafters and to which external rainwater guttering is fixed.

Feather
To wear away or smooth an edge until it is undetectable.

Galvanized
Covered with a protective coating of zinc.

Gel
A substance with a thick jelly-like consistency.

Grain
The general direction of wood fibres. *or* The pattern produced on the surface of timber by cutting through the fibres.

Hardwood
Timber cut from deciduous trees.

Header face
The end of a house brick.

Key
To abrade or incise a surface to provide a better grip when gluing something to it or painting over it.

Knotting
A shellac-based sealer used to prevent softwood resin bleeding through a coat of paint.

Lath and plaster
A method of finishing a timber-framed wall or ceiling. Narrow strips of wood are nailed to the wall studs or joists to provide a supporting framework for the plaster.

Mastic
A commercially prepared non-setting compound used to seal joints.

Moisture-vapour permeable
Used to describe a finish which allows timber to dry out while protecting it from rainwater.

Muntin
A central vertical member of a panel door.

Oxidize
To form a layer of metal oxide as in rusting.

Papier mâché
A stiff filler made by mashing newsprint (newspaper) in warm water mixed with wallpaper paste.

Plasterboard
A wall-cladding material comprising a core of aerated gypsum plaster covered on both sides with a strong paper lining.

Primary colours
The three pure colours – red, blue and yellow.

Primer
The first coat of a traditional paint system. A primer protects the workpiece and reduces absorption of subsequent coats.

Profile
The outline or contour of an object.

Riser
The vertical part of a step.

Rubber
A pad of cotton wool wrapped in soft cloth used to apply stain or shellac polish.

Running bond
The pattern formed by bricks laid with their vertical joints staggered regularly. Also known as stretcher bond.

Scribe
To copy the profile of a surface on the edge of sheet material which is to be butted against it. *or* To mark a line with a pointed tool.

Shellac
A substance exuded by the lac insect. It is dissolved in industrial alcohol to make French polish.

Slipstone
A small teardrop-section sharpening stone used to hone the cutting edges of woodworking gouges.

Softwood
Timber cut from coniferous trees.

Stile
A vertical member of a door, window sash or ladder.

Stopper
A wood filler which matches the colour of the timber.

Stretcher face
The long face of a house brick.

String
A board which runs from one floor level to another and into which staircase treads and risers are jointed. The one on the open side of a staircase is an open string, the one against the wall is known as a wall string.

Stud partition
An interior timber-framed dividing wall.

Studs
The vertical members of a timber-framed wall.

Template
A cut-out pattern to help shape a workpiece accurately.

Thinners
A solvent used to dilute paint or varnish.

Thixotropic
A property of some paints which have a jelly-like consistency until stirred or applied, at which point they become liquid.

Top coat
The outer layer of paint.

Transom
A horizontal dividing member of a window frame.

Tread
The horizontal part of a step.

Undercoat
A layer of paint used to obliterate the colour of a primer and to build a protective body of paint prior to the application of a top coat.

Weatherboarding
Exterior wooden wall cladding.

Wood-boring insects
Beetles with larvae that feed on wood fibres. The most common variety is the furniture beetle or woodworm.